Jules Verne

JULES VERNE

 The Man
Who Invented Tomorrow

PEGGY TEETERS

Walker and Company ◆ New York

First published in the United States of America in 1992
by Walker Publishing Company, Inc.

Published simultaneously in Canada by Thomas Allen & Son
Canada, Limited, Markham, Ontario

Library of Congress Cataloging-in-Publication Data
Teeters, Peggy.
Jules Verne: the man who invented tomorrow / Peggy Teeters.
p.   cm.
Includes bibliographical references and index.
Summary: Examines the life and work of the nineteenth-century
French writer whose fantastic novels took his readers to all of the
places he had dreamed about as a young boy.
ISBN 0-8027-8189-6 (cloth). —ISBN 0-8027-8191-8 (rein)
1. Verne, Jules, 1828–1905—Biography—Juvenile literature.
2. Authors, French—19th century—Biography—Juvenile literature.
[1. Verne, Jules, 1828–1905.   2. Authors, French.]   I. Title.
PQ2469.Z5T44   1993
843'.8—dc20   92-35457
CIP
AC

Frontispiece photograph appears courtesy of the Dublin Library.

Book design by Georg Brewer

Printed in the United States of America

2   4   6   8   10   9   7   5   3   1

Contents

Contents

Jules Verne

1

THE RUNAWAY

▼

On a summer morning in 1839 in the town of Chantenay, France, Jules Verne awoke with only one thought in his mind: He was going to run away from home. After all, he was almost twelve and it was time to see the world.

He lay there for a moment dreaming of the adventures ahead. Soon he'd be aboard the *Coralie,* a three-masted schooner headed for the West Indies, and in a few weeks he'd be exploring mysterious jungles filled with weird plants and animals waiting to devour him. Not too far away, he'd find deep caves beckoning to him to come in and discover secret passageways. Maybe he'd never find his way back. His heart pounded at the thought. From the ship he'd peer down into the sea and find terrible monsters reaching up to grab him with their tentacles. Many of these creatures were drawings in his copybook, his prized possession. Now he would see them come to life.

He slipped out of bed, trying not to make any noise. His younger brother, Paul, was in the bed next to his. Accidentally he dropped a shoe, and Paul set up wondering what had made the noise. Jules didn't move a muscle. A few seconds later, his brother fell asleep again. Jules finished dressing and stuffed some clothes into a small canvas bag. He tiptoed out of the bedroom and down the stairs to the kitchen. Here he found some cheese and bread and threw them in with his clothing. As he headed for the kitchen door, he stood there for a moment and thought about his family. When would he see them again? In many months? In many years? Or maybe never? He loved them all, even his three little sisters, who were nuisances at times. A lump came to his throat as he remembered that this was the day his father was going to read from *Robinson Crusoe*, his favorite book. His father read to the children every night after supper. But there was no turning back. He was out to have adventures of his own.

He closed the door ever so gently and then raced down the hill toward the harbor at Nantes where the *Coralie* was anchored. He had gone there yesterday just to look at her and dream, but something unexpected had happened. He had met a cabin boy on the schooner who didn't want to go to the West Indies. The two boys had talked for a while, and Jules tried to persuade him to let him take his place on the ship. At first the boy said he couldn't do it, but after Jules gave him some money, he finally agreed. They made plans to meet at the same place on the dock at six o'clock the next morning.

As Jules raced down the road toward Nantes clutching his bag of food and clothing, he was tempted to pinch himself to make sure he wasn't dreaming. He came back to reality in a hurry when he heard some shutters opening and a voice calling his name. It was Mathurine, his old nurse, who now owned a small butcher shop. He mumbled something but kept on running. Nothing could stop him now. He would just have to hope that she wouldn't tell his father. Come to think of it, she hadn't the slightest idea that he was headed for the West Indies. He was sure that she believed he was meeting one of his friends.

When Jules reached the dock, the cabin boy was already there. The two of them got into a small rowboat and headed for the ship. As the boat bobbed up and down on the choppy sea, Jules thought about the fun he and Paul had had last summer learning to sail. There were times when they had almost drowned, but the next day they were there again, determined to master the skills of sailing. The two of them loved the sea.

Jules informed the captain of the *Coralie* that he had never been on a ship before. But he told him that he knew how to sail and that he was sure he could learn the duties of a cabin boy. The captain must have been impressed with the tall, red-headed young fellow standing before him. Jules looked so eager and excited that the man hired him at once. He then gave Jules his first job: washing dishes in the galley. The new cabin boy was so thrilled with being on the *Coralie* that without a word he went to work on the mountain of plates and cups.

In the meantime, the Verne household was in an uproar. Jules was missing, and no one knew where he was. Paul said he had seen Jules getting out of bed early in the morning while it was still dark. Or had he dreamed it? He wasn't sure. M. Verne wanted to know where he could be going at such an early hour. He pounded on the kitchen table as he spoke, and Paul could see how furious he was. No one answered him. No one knew where Jules had gone. He had never disappeared before.

M. Verne decided to talk to his neighbors and the people in town. He banged the kitchen door as he left and headed down the road that Jules had taken early that morning. He had a feeling that his older son had decided once and for all to see the places he had only read about. But would he actually run away from his home and family? M. Verne's anger turned to a kind of sadness. He knew that this son was the dreamer in the family who yearned for adventure and wanted to see the world now—not later. But he had never expected him to run away.

When M. Verne went into town, he stopped at the butcher shop run by Mathurine, Jules's old nurse. She told him that she had seen his son early in the morning crossing the church square and running toward Nantes. M. Verne hurried over to the seaport town, and after asking some sailors if they had seen a red-headed boy around the dock that morning, he had a word of encouragement. One of the men said he had seen two boys in a dinghy rowing out to the *Coralie*, which had already left for the Indies. When he saw the stricken look on M. Verne's face, he told him that if he hurried, he could take the steam ferry that would get him to Paimboeuf, the last port of call before the *Coralie* reached the open sea.

Jules's father managed to get on board the ferry just in time and prayed that he could get to Paimboeuf before the ship sailed for the Indies. He was in luck. When he arrived in Paimboeuf, he clambered aboard the schooner and soon found the captain. He told him what had happened and that he had come to take his son back home. The captain found Jules and reluctantly handed him over to his angry father. He told M. Verne that he believed his son could have become an excellent cabin boy.

On the trip back, Pierre Verne kept asking Jules why he had done such a thing and worried his whole family. Jules hung his head and didn't answer. How could he tell his practical father that every day he thought about adventures in the sea or in the sky or even in the center of the earth? How could he admit that he hated school and especially the Latin lessons he had to take that summer to get a better grade? And how could he explain that he could never be content just doing ordinary things?

When the two of them arrived home, the entire family rushed over to Jules. His mother gave him a big hug and begged him never to run away again. But his father took him upstairs and whipped him. He told him there would be no supper for him that night and that he had to stay in his bedroom until morning.

The next day Mme Verne knocked on Jules's door, and when he opened it, she put her arms around him. She made him promise that from now on, he would travel only in his imagination.

Jules Verne did just that. In later years, he wrote fantastic novels that took his readers to all of the places he had dreamed about when he was a young boy.

2

JULES AND PAUL

▼

Jules Verne was born on February 8, 1828, in Nantes, France. He was the oldest of five children; the others were his brother, Paul, and three sisters, Mathilde, Anna, and Marie.

The Verne household was a happy one. Pierre Verne, the father, was a successful lawyer, quite strict but fair. He was interested in poetry and classical music and did his best to keep up with the latest news in science. Sophie Verne, the mother, came from a background of men connected with the sea and secretly wished that her boys would become sailors. She was known for her lively imagination. People said that Jules inherited this trait from her, along with her red hair.

When Jules and Paul were young boys, they spent many hours on the quais, or docks, near their home. Here they fished for bleak and other small fish or simply stood there and watched the ships passing by on their way to the open sea. On some days, they went to the Quai Brancas to visit the birdcatcher whose cages held tropical birds from South America, Africa, and the West Indies. Sometimes they were lucky enough to meet up with an old sea captain who would tell them true stories and tall tales about his travels.

Jules's first school, the Dame School, was run by Mme Sambin. She was the widow of a sea captain, and the boys and girls heard the same story again and again of what happened to her thirty years ago: Her husband had left one morning after their honeymoon and never returned. But Jules never snickered when she mentioned the tragic tale at least once a day. Instead, he sat there and wondered what happened to Captain Sambin. Did he become a kind of Sinbad the Sailor, destined to sail the seven seas and encounter one disaster after another? Or did he get shipwrecked on a desert island like Robinson Crusoe? Would he then come home some day with a man Friday and a parrot?

Mme Sambin's tragic story must have made quite an impression on six-year-old Jules. Fifty years later, in 1891, he wrote a novel called *Mistress Branican* that told about a woman whose husband went off on a sailing ship and never came back. But it had a different twist. Mistress Branican went looking for her husband. She searched the coral seas of the Pacific for fourteen years and finally found him — alive.

Jules stayed in the Dame School for three years and learned reading, writing, and arithmetic. When he was nine, he moved on to St. Stanislaus School, where he excelled in Latin, Greek, geography, and singing. His teachers later recalled him as "a slender boy with hair all awry, running on stilts, throwing himself passionately into all forms of sport, a real king of the playground."[1] A few years later, he began attending the Lycée Royal where, except for geography, his grades went downhill.

His time at the Lycée turned out to be a constant struggle after the first summer he spent in a cottage that his father bought at Chantenay by the Loire River when he was ten years old. While at the cottage that summer, Jules lived in a different world, where his imagination was free to roam. From the window of his small room he could see the river and the wide meadows that were flooded during winter. In summer, there were small islands in the Loire, and one morning in July, Jules decided to go to one of them below Chantenay. He didn't invite Paul to go with him; this was an adventure he had to experience all alone. He wanted to see what it felt like to be shipwrecked on an island and pretend to be Robinson Crusoe.

When he arrived on the island, he went to work at once building a hut out of twigs and branches. When he was finished, he crept in and had no trouble imagining that he was a castaway and far away from home. As he checked out the tiny strip of land, he could see that no one else was in sight. Then again, could a strange creature be hidden in that clump of bushes about thirty feet away? He felt a chill race up and down his spine and hurried back to his little shack. But it wasn't fear that made him leave a short time later. He discovered that he was hungry, and when the hunger pains became intense, he rushed home as soon as the tide went down and walked in as the family sat down to supper. He never tried being shipwrecked again.

That first summer at Chantenay, he and Paul got up early, ate breakfast in the kitchen with their little sisters, did their chores, and then headed for the river. Here they would get on board their makeshift raft and push off into the world of adventure. What lay around the bend in the river? Could a pirate be waiting for them, ready to capture them and seize their raft? Every day was a challenge as they went into the unknown.

This was also the time when Jules and Paul learned how to sail. The two boys were crazy about boats and they often rented leaky old tubs for a franc a day. Sixty years later in a magazine article, Jules wrote:

What hopeless sailors we were! Tacking downriver on the ebb tide against the westerly breeze, how many times we capsized disgracefully owing to a misguided shove at the helm, a botched maneuver, an ill-advised tug on the sheets when a swell arose to ruffle the waters of the Loire River. We generally set out with the descending tide and returned on the flood tide a few hours later. And as our hired boat floundered along between the shores, we cast looks of envy on the pretty pleasure yachts skimming past and around us.[2]

Eventually the two boys became so skilled that they went from a one-sail boat to a three-master.

The next year, Jules tried to sail on the *Coralie*. His parents had never realized that along with Paul, Jules, too, heard the siren call of the sea, but in a different way. Paul had plans to become master of his own ship someday, but Jules wanted to travel to distant lands and explore them.

During Jules's last two years at the Lycée, he discovered the magic in books. At first he practically devoured the romance novels he could find, and many nights he read these books instead of doing his homework. At this time France was going through the romantic period, which emphasized the imagination and emotions instead of reason and intellect. Poets and romance writers became very popular, and historical love stories appealed to many people. As time went on, Jules abandoned his romance novels and came home with books that had more substance.

Two books had an especially profound effect on him. The first was *The Hunchback of Notre Dame* by Victor Hugo, a romance of medieval times that centers around a deformed bell ringer who is in love with a Gypsy girl and tries to save her from an angry mob that claims she is a witch. The second was *The Three Musketeers* by Alexandre

Dumas, a story that features three brave young men who will "do or die" for honor and glory. This swashbuckling tale of adventure appealed to the young Jules and once again kept him from doing his school assignments.

At this time Jules also enjoyed reading stories by foreign writers such as Sir Walter Scott and Edgar Allan Poe. He was intrigued by one of Poe's short stories called "A Descent into the Maelstrom," in which a giant whirlpool at sea spins so fast that it pulls ships and men right down into it and destroys them. Jules was also impressed with Poe's knowledge of science and the universe.

Jules tried his hand at writing love poems. At first he hesitated showing them to Paul and his close friends, but when he did one day, he was pleased to hear that they weren't too bad. When he was sixteen, he turned out a long, tragic drama in verse that he read at a family gathering one Sunday afternoon. His cousins listened—and laughed. They thought it was supposed to be humorous. That night, completely humiliated, he burned the pages and never tried that kind of writing again.

At the age of sixteen, Jules finished his schooling at the Lycée along with his classmates. He then began to study law at home under his father's guidance. He hated every minute of it. Then in the spring of 1847, when he was nineteen, Jules received an unexpected reprieve from his law studies. His father told him that he could go to Paris to live with his great-aunt and get ready for his first-year law exams at the Sorbonne, the University of Paris. But Pierre had another reason for sending him away at that time. He had learned that Caroline, Jules's first cousin, was going to get married, and he knew that his son would be heartbroken when he heard the news. Jules had been in love with this pretty girl from the time he was eleven, even though she had ignored his romantic notes and poems through the years. In fact, there had been occasions when she had laughed at his attempts to woo her and reminded him that she was two years older and much more experienced in the ways of the world.

Jules went to Paris, passed his examinations, and came back to Nantes to study his law books again in his father's office. But he sat at his desk some days thinking about Paris and making plans to return. He knew that in this fabulous city he could truly become a writer and win fame and fortune. All he had to do was figure out a way to convince his father.

☞ 3 ☜

PARIS, WONDERFUL PARIS!

▼

Jules did his best to become interested in his law books, but no matter how hard he tried, his thoughts strayed to Paris. Paris! What a city! People came from all over to see its famous landmarks: Notre Dame cathedral, the Arc de Triomphe, and the Louvre museum, formerly the king's palace. Paris was also known for its artists and musicians and theaters. It had produced great writers, including Victor Hugo and Alexandre Dumas, whose latest books were bringing them wide acclaim. Could he, Jules Verne, ever write anything as spellbinding as Hugo's *The Hunchback of Notre Dame* or Dumas's *The Count of Monte Cristo*? He decided that he had a chance—if he moved to the place of his dreams.

Jules realized that it was wise not to antagonize his father by asking him almost every day if he could leave home for a while. It would be better to become more interested in family matters instead of always reading. The first thing he did was to notice what his little sisters were doing, and when he paid attention to Anna playing the piano, he couldn't believe his ears. She was amazing with her talent, and he had an idea she was a child prodigy.

Another time he persuaded Paul to join him in playing some piano duets, but when his family groaned at their efforts, he laughed good-naturedly. Some nights he took part in the skits the family did after supper, and he outdid himself in every dramatic scene, pretending he was on stage in one of the plays now being performed in Paris.

One morning Jules had an unexpected shock. Paul told him that he had signed up with a merchant ship that was sailing to the Reunion Islands off the coast of Africa. He would be leaving December 23 and would get back the next September. Paul said that he wished Jules could go with him.

Jules said nothing. He and Paul both knew that the older son was expected automatically to follow in his father's footsteps. It didn't matter that Jules wasn't a bit interested in law. For a fleeting moment, he felt a twinge of jealousy when he thought about his brother's freedom in choosing to become a sea captain or anything else he desired. But Jules had to admit that Paul had his problems, too. He had tried to get into the French Naval Academy and had flunked the exam. Signing on with a merchant ship as an apprentice was the next-best thing for now. Someday Paul would reach his goal of becoming a sea captain, no matter how many years it took.

After Paul's news, Jules tried to figure a way to persuade Pierre Verne to let him return to Paris for his second exam. He couldn't believe it when he learned that his parents had already decided he should go there to study for the next phase of his training in the law. Jules went around in a state of shock and elation and put aside his little dramatic speech. He had been all set to tell his parents that right now his whole life and future were at stake and that he would be a failure if he didn't get to Paris. He was sure, however, that his little emotional plea would come in handy when he planned to move to Paris permanently. This was not the time to tell them that.

Then something unexpected happened. A short time after Jules's twentieth birthday, on February 8, 1848, King Louis Philippe was forced to give up his throne, and the Second Republic was declared. For the first time in France, all the people were given the right to vote, and a group of lawmakers was elected. Later, a temporary government came into being. But more trouble broke out in June, and fifty thousand workers fought in the Paris streets with soldiers. At least ten thousand of the workers were killed. Eventually, a new constitution was drawn up and things began to quiet down. Jules thought for a while that his father wouldn't allow him to leave, but when the fighting stopped, he was on his way. This time he stayed with his cousin Henri because his great-aunt had fled the city when the revolution broke out.

Once again Jules passed his exam with a fair grade. He then headed for Chantenay, where he would spend the summer. He felt happy and inspired after his short stay in Paris and wrote a humorous one-act play called *Une Promenade en Mer* ("A Walk on the Sea") and three outlines of lighthearted story ideas suitable for the stage. But another reason for his feeling that all was right with the world was a conversation he had one morning with his father at the breakfast table. They had discussed the importance of the third law exam, and Jules had pointed out that the exam questions at the Sorbonne were keyed to the lectures. How could he hear them if he studied at home? He almost fell off his chair when Pierre Verne quietly agreed with him. What also helped was the backing from Paul, who was home for a short time, and the rest of his family. This was it. He, Jules Verne, was again going to Paris, where he would study, of course, and where he would soon become a famous playwright. What was different about this trip was that he would be living there, not just staying for short periods.

On November 10, 1849, Jules and his good friend Edouard Bonamy set out for their new home. Bundled up in greatcoats and scarves, they said farewell to their families and climbed into the stagecoach. The two young men were in a hurry. They wanted to reach the city in three days, arriving on a Sunday night to witness a special ceremony—the inauguration of the new government.

At this time, the National Assembly was to hold a civic and religious ceremony in the open on the Place de la Concorde. The new constitution would be read, and the Archbishop of Paris would lead the Te Deum. Jules knew he'd be witnessing a part of history. They were so eager to see all of this that when they reached Tours, they tried to get on the special train taking the National Guard of the region to Paris. An alert soldier spotted them, asked them questions, and told them they were in danger of getting arrested. Jules and Edouard quietly disappeared into the crowd at the station.

They reached Paris after dark. The city was covered with snow and looked so beautiful that they decided to walk in order to find a room. They were thrilled at the thought of living here, and their enthusiasm propelled them along the streets. But after being turned down at one boarding house after another, they became discouraged. When they finally found an apartment with two rooms on the top floor of a rickety old house, they knew they probably couldn't do much better. At least they would be living on the Left Bank of the Seine River, famous for its artists and writers. This was the old part of the city, filled with quaint homes and crowded streets and many intriguing little shops. This section was also ideal for Jules; the Sorbonne was within walking distance of his boarding house.

Three days later, Edouard wrote a letter to his family. Part of it read:

> Reaching Paris only on Sunday night, all we saw of this much talked of celebration of the Constitution were the last candles guttering in their sockets. The Concorde was a basilica of velvet and gold above a forecourt of snow. After trudging many streets and climbing many flights of stairs, we finally discovered two suitable rooms at 24 Rue de l'Ancienne Comédie, at thirty francs a month.[3]

One morning Jules looked around his shabby room and had to admit it was nothing compared to his room back home. But it really didn't matter. Here he would make his future. Here he would write his plays and become famous. He could see the people flocking to the theater to enjoy the latest creation of young Jules Verne. Nothing could stop him now!

4

A Bump in the Night

▼

A few days later, Jules and Edouard went to see Mme Arnous-Rivière, an old family friend from Nantes who was now established in Paris. They had made arrangements to send their baggage to her house since they didn't have a forwarding address at the time. Jules tried not to be rude, but he made some kind of excuse to leave after a few minutes in order to get back to the boarding house. He could hardly wait to check over his manuscripts to see if they had all arrived in good condition. Nothing else mattered; those papers were his whole life, and nothing must happen to them.

The moment Jules arrived in his room, he unpacked the manuscripts and found that they had arrived intact. He placed some of his writings on the narrow bed and tried to look them over with a cold, critical eye. Not bad, he thought, not bad. Would he be able to sell them? He knew there were many young writers in Paris hoping to win fame and fortune, but he honestly felt that he had a good chance too. He believed in his talents and felt that some day others would recognize them and buy his articles and plays and poems.

As he sat on the bed, he glanced around his shabby attic room. It's a good thing my mother can't see this place, he thought. All it contained were two small beds, a small work table, two wooden chairs, and a tall cabinet for his clothes. A small fireplace was over in one corner, but Jules was sure he would never be able to afford the firewood during the cold winter months. He kept on rereading his material, and when Edouard walked in a little later, Jules looked up and said, "They'll see one day what stuff he was made of, this poor young man they knew as Jules Verne."[4] If he doesn't starve to death first, he wanted to add, but didn't. He had to keep on believing that great things were going to happen to him or he wouldn't be able to write anything.

As the two of them settled in with their few belongings, they decided to look up Hignard, an old friend who had come to Paris several months earlier to start a career in music. He would be able to show them the city and point out the restaurants that had good food for a reasonable price. Jules and Edouard had already discovered that the monthly allowances given to them by their fathers just wasn't enough. M. Verne had told Jules that he would have to live on one hundred francs a month and that he knew other young men who managed quite well on that amount of money. Jules told him that his expenses for rent and meals left him with practically nothing left over to see a play or buy some books. His father answered that it could be done if he doled out his allowance very carefully.

Jules tried one more time and wrote another letter back home in which he itemized his bills and told his parents that often he had to survive on only one meal a day. He told them that for the last week he couldn't even do that. He had existed on dried prunes and water. He admitted that in a way it had been his fault. He had spent sixteen francs on a special volume of Shakespeare that beckoned to him from a bookstore window. "I'm absolutely famished for books," he wrote. "It makes my fingers itch just to look at the bookshop counters."[5]

It was probably Sophie Verne who persuaded her husband to increase her son's allowance. She no doubt pictured Jules reduced to skin and bones in his little attic room in Paris. She had heard of artists living there who had literally starved to death. M. Verne finally agreed to add twenty-five more francs to Jules's monthly sum but told his wife that he had no intention of sending any more and that Jules had to stop being extravagant. Jules, of course, was grateful for the extra money but knew that he would still have problems paying the bills and would suffer from hunger pangs fairly often.

One Sunday afternoon when Edouard went to visit another friend, Jules decided to visit the Cathedral of Notre Dame. Ever since reading Victor Hugo's magnificent novel *The Hunchback of Notre Dame*, Jules had been entranced with Hugo's plot. Why would such a famous poet give a building of this kind such an important role in his book? He soon had his answer.

When he arrived at Notre Dame, he stood in front and stared. It was unbelievable. Not only was it overwhelming in its Gothic grandeur dating back to the twelfth century but it created a feeling of awe as he looked it over. He noticed at once the famous rose window over the middle door and decided to enter through there, knowing that something was special about the window, something he couldn't explain. When he went in, he couldn't see a thing. It was pitch dark. As his eyes became adjusted, he groped his way to a pew and slipped into it, almost believing that he had stepped back in time to a century belonging to the Middle Ages.

He sat there quietly, absorbing his surroundings. He could see an altar at the far end with red flowers and tall white candles and statues of saints in alcoves on each side of the church. He thought about Victor Hugo and how all of this must have impressed the man and inspired him to write his famous novel. Jules remembered his characters, especially Esmerelda, the Gypsy girl, and Quasimodo, the hunchback. Poor Quasimodo! He was so deformed with his crooked back and his large head, one eye, and shock of red hair. . . . His daydreaming stopped abruptly. Someone behind him had placed a hand on his left shoulder. When he turned around, would he see one monstrous eye staring at him? He finally looked behind him and found a young priest handing him a pamphlet. He took it, thanked him, and hurried out into the normal, everyday world.

When he left the cathedral, he was tempted to visit the Louvre art museum to see the *Mona Lisa*, Leonardo da Vinci's famous painting. But he decided against it. He had heard that the best time to go there was early in the morning or late in the afternoon in order to avoid the long lines of people. He would have to go there on another Sunday. He would do it soon because he admired this artist not only for his paintings but also for his interest in science and for his notebooks filled with drawings of unique machines. Some looked like the airplanes that wouldn't make their appearance for another four hundred years or more. Some of Jules's notebooks also contained sketches of this kind, many drawn when he was eight or nine years old.

Later that afternoon, he remembered that he had a social event to go to in a very fashionable part of town and that it was his turn to wear the set of evening clothes that he and Edouard shared. Fortunately, neither one was upset over this arrangement, and they often joked about it when they were out with their friends. At this party, as at most of these parties, Jules grew bored when the conversation turned to politics. After spending most of his time around the buffet table, repeatedly filling his plate with gourmet food made by the best chefs in Paris, Jules began to feel uncomfortable. He knew it was time to thank his hostess for her hospitality and head for home.

When he reached the large, luxurious staircase that led down to the front door, he became fascinated by the marble banister. Without hesitating, he straddled it and slid down like a three-year-old. His ride came to an abrupt halt when he bumped into something with such force that he was sent sprawling on the steps. That something turned out to be a giant of a man innocently going up the stairs to the party in the dining room. Horrified, Jules apologized repeatedly.

His "victim" stood up and told him that he was fine. His only concern was that he hoped the Nantes omelet he had just eaten was still there. He laughed and patted his huge stomach. Jules wondered if he had actually heard this man say these words. He, Jules, was known for this special omelet recipe and told the man about it. Jules also mentioned that his creation would win praise from the best chefs in Paris. The man smiled and said he'd have to try it. Could he come to his place next Monday? All he had to bring was the recipe. Jules gulped but accepted the invitation, knowing he could do a great job. He asked the man for his name and address, and when the portly gentleman answered him, Jules felt faint. It was the author Alexandre Dumas, the rage of Paris!

5

THE GREAT DUMAS

▼

Jules spent several restless nights after his meeting with Dumas. He often woke up in a panic. Why did he accept that invitation to show off his Nantes omelet recipe? Suppose it stuck to the pan? Or he forgot an ingredient? On top of that, he had recently heard that not only was cooking one of Dumas's favorite hobbies but that Dumas himself was an outstanding chef.

On that Monday morning, Jules arose at dawn to do some more work on a play. Later, he paid a quick visit to a bookstore nearby to find out about where Dumas lived. He was impressed to hear that he owned a chateau on the outskirts of Paris and that he called the place Monte Cristo after his famous novel. There were always many guests and visitors.

Even though Jules was prepared for a home that was out of the ordinary, he marveled at what he saw when he arrived at Monte Cristo. The chateau looked like a fairy-tale castle, complete with Gothic towers and turrets, and was nestled among tall elm trees. Peacocks strutted across the elegant lawns, and swans swam on artificial lakes that dotted the landscape.

Eventually Jules made his way into the immense kitchen, where he found Dumas dressed in an apron and chef's cap. He was reading a cookbook, but he shut it when Jules walked in. He gave Jules a cup of coffee and then took him over to a work table where all kinds of utensils were on hand and told him he was ready for the great omelet. Dumas laughed when Jules took from his coat pocket a small envelope, saying it contained a special herb that was an important part of the recipe.

A half hour later, both men were seated at the elegant dining room table enjoying Jules's creation. Dumas exclaimed that it was delicious, simply delicious, and that he must add this recipe to his collection of recipes from all over the world. Could Jules tell him what the secret ingredient was? Never mind, he added. A good cook should never give away his little gourmet touches. After eating the Nantes omelet, Dumas took Jules on a guided tour of the chateau. Room after room was furnished with expensive furniture, Oriental rugs, and beautiful paintings. They then went outside, where Jules saw a stable for Dumas's horses, an aviary for his collection of tropical birds, and a monkey house for the amusement of his guests. Later, Dumas took him to a small island in one of the artificial lakes. The only thing on the island was a stone pavilion containing a single room. Dumas informed Jules that he wrote his plays and novels here and that visitors were never allowed to come in. He had to have complete silence when he wrote. Jules was impressed by his words. This huge extrovert of a man who liked people and parties had to be in a quiet place when he wrote.

Before Jules left Monte Cristo, he confided to Dumas that he hoped to become a playwright someday. He also said that he really wasn't doing well and had decided to try another kind of writing. Could Dumas spare the time to teach him some of the basics of writing historical novels that seemed so popular these days? Dumas answered that he would be happy to teach his young friend how to write a story that would sell. Jules would have to come to the chateau for several hours a week.

After visiting Dumas for a month, Jules began to write a novel. Every morning he made himself sit at a small table in his room and write from 6:00 A.M. until noon. But no matter how hard he tried, his love scenes sounded awkward and silly, and he himself found the whole thing boring. He kept at it for another month and finally admitted he couldn't create the proper swashbuckling atmosphere or tone that he found in Dumas's stories. Jules had to try something else—but what?

On one of his visits to the chateau, Jules received an unexpected invitation. Dumas asked him to attend the gala reopening of his Théatre Historique on the Boulevard du Temple. The theater, owned by Dumas, had closed during the revolution of 1848, along with many others in Paris. Jules was delighted to be asked, and so on the evening of February 21, 1849, he was among the invited guests sitting in Alexandre Dumas's private box. He wrote about it in his next letter to his parents: "Last night I went to the first performance of *The Youth of the Musketeers*. I was in Alexandre Dumas's box. . . . I saw a lot of well-known people. These little privileges are not to be scorned."[6]

That year Jules managed to write two historical plays, after much agonizing over scenes that to him sounded wooden and dull. He also worked on a humorous, lighthearted play. His two good friends, Edouard and Aristide, read all three works and liked them. This gave Jules the courage to show them to Dumas.

He was surprised when Dumas singled out the comedy. In fact, he told Jules that he would like to produce it in his theater. Oh, yes, it needed some revisions here and there, but on the whole it showed genuine talent. Jules was overwhelmed. He had hoped for some kind of support ever since their friendship began, but never did he dream that the famous writer would snap up one of his little plays.

Jules rewrote some of the lines, and *Broken Straws* opened on June 12, 1850, in the well-known theater that belonged to Dumas. Many of Jules's friends were there, and Dumas himself brought a large group from Monte Cristo. A classmate of Jules from Nantes, a rich one, offered to publish the play in book form. M. and Mme Verne were not in the audience because Jules hadn't told them about the performance. He couldn't let his father spoil such a wonderful event.

The play went over very well. The audience roared with laughter in all the right places and gave the young playwright a standing ovation when the curtain came down. Some of the Parisian critics said that Jules Verne had a real flair for comedy. Although the play ran for twelve nights, it was not long enough for him to make any money. But he knew that he had a modest success on his hands. Dumas agreed with him and told him so.

After *Broken Straws* had finished its run, Jules sent a copy of the printed version to his father. He received an angry letter from him saying that he was wasting his time on such trivial material. Worse than that, said Pierre Verne, the play centered around a flirtatious wife and a not-too-bright husband. What sort of people was he associating with in Paris? He ordered Jules to spend every available minute on his law studies—now!

Jules had a hard time understanding how upset his father was. After all, the play was a comedy, a harmless farce meant to make people laugh at the witty lines and situations. His mother, on the other hand, came to her son's defense and told her husband that he was too stuffy and serious. She also said she was thrilled that her son's play had been produced in Paris. That was an accomplishment in itself.

A short time later, the director of the Nantes Municipal Theater wrote to Jules and suggested that *Broken Straws* be presented in the playwright's hometown. Jules asked his parents for permission to do so and couldn't believe their answer. They said yes, and Jules never knew that his father had consented only because he was afraid that his son would abruptly stop going to his law classes if the answer was otherwise.

Jules came home two days before the play was presented in Nantes on November 7, 1850. He had the pleasure of going with his parents to see it and was thrilled when it was a huge success. The hometown audience enjoyed itself immensely. When the curtain came down, he was given a standing ovation.

When Jules returned to Paris, his friend Aristide introduced him to a group of young men who had formed a science club. They would sit around every Saturday night and discuss a variety of subjects. One time they talked about the inaccuracies in some of Edgar Allan Poe's scientific tales. Another night they had a heated argument about the science of the future. During this period, Jules began to visit his cousin Henri Garcet, a professor of mathematics who was learned in other subjects as well. The two men met often, and Jules listened intently as Henri explained the basic laws of mechanics and discussed the latest discoveries in astronomy and technology. Whenever Jules had a free day, he went to the public libraries, where he could read the excellent scientific magazines and bulletins of the various organizations in the science field. He put down much of this information in a notebook that soon overflowed with facts that made fascinating reading and that he would use in his adventure novels later on.

Despite the time Jules was now spending discussing and

reading about science, his friendship with Dumas grew even stronger. One day when he went out to Monte Cristo, he confided to Dumas that he had to begin making some money. His plays weren't doing much to help him meet expenses. Maybe he could try a new field of literature. Why couldn't he do a series of novels using the theme of man against nature? It wasn't a new idea, of course, but Jules's stories would be different. Dumas and Sir Walter Scott wrote novels based on past events, so why couldn't he, Jules, look to the future? A new world was being created by modern science and technology, and it was time to have an explorer, a scientist, or an aeronaut as the hero instead of a knight on a white horse. That person would be armed with the latest inventions or scientific knowledge instead of a sword.

Dumas was more than enthusiastic. He urged Jules to begin at once to jot down these ideas before they escaped him. Dumas called these novels "the literature of the future." He told Jules to cut down on his hours of sleep and not to waste a single minute. Everything must center around his writing. Only by following this discipline had Dumas been able to write four hundred stories and plays in twenty years.

Jules went home all aglow. He was about to undertake a new kind of writing. He said it out loud: "The literature of the future." It had a nice ring to it, and he'd always be grateful to Dumas for his encouragement. But he wished that this powerful and rich man had given him a grant and asked him to write material for him, the great Dumas. That money right now would buy the books in the scientific field that he needed in his new venture. Good old Shakespeare couldn't help now.

Several days later, Jules came up with several chapters of an idea he had for his first adventure book set in the future. He had to show them to Dumas. One afternoon after his law classes, he hurried over to Monte Cristo. When he got there, he couldn't believe what he saw. Creditors were running all over the place and seizing the furnishings. Some of them were posting labels on the pieces to be sold at auction. A handful of young writers were standing around looking bewildered and upset. Jules asked one of them what was going on. The young man told him that M. Dumas was bankrupt and, according to the latest report, had left Paris. No one knew where he was.

6

A JOB IN THE THEATER

▼

The next morning Jules awakened and wondered if his visit to Monte Cristo had been only a bad dream. He knew it was true when Edouard told him that afternoon that he, too, had heard about the creditors swarming all over Dumas's estate.

Jules was stunned for days. How could this great man and writer suddenly be penniless? He was certain that Dumas's generosity toward young writers and poets, along with his extravagant ways, had been responsible.

Jules concluded that the best thing for him to do at the moment was to throw himself into the study of the law so he could pass his final examination. He mustn't disappoint his father or the rest of his family by failing after several years of classes and lectures.

In the meantime, Dumas's theater was taken over by Jules Seveste, who renamed it the Lyric Theater. Seveste announced that he wanted to produce a series of light operettas. Jules had been working on the libretto—the text— for one and quickly finished it so that he could offer it to the new owner. He was delighted when Seveste accepted his material and produced it two months later. But the operetta had only twenty performances, and once again Jules's hopes of becoming well known in the theater were put on hold.

A short time later, he took his final law exam and passed it by only a few points. His father sent him a letter of congratulations and told him that he was looking forward to renaming the law firm Pierre Verne et Fils—Pierre Verne and Son. Jules felt trapped, but he knew one thing for sure. He was not going back to Nantes. He didn't want to spend the rest of his days in a small town working as a lawyer. Never! Never! Never! He'd rather be dead and buried. Right now, he had to concentrate on finding a job in Paris; any kind of job would do.

Eventually Jules was in desperate need of money. He tutored law students for their exams, but this paid him practically nothing. He later took on a job as a clerk in a law office, but once again, it paid very little and took many hours away from his writing. It was then that he made up his mind never to associate himself again with the law, even though he was now a qualified lawyer.

While working at these little jobs, Jules managed to write three scientific articles slanted toward young readers. He sent them off to juvenile magazines and was pleased when all of them were published. Maybe he had found his niche. Maybe he should simply stay with this kind of article writing. There seemed to be a ready market out there eager to accept his work. But with great reluctance, he admitted to himself that he'd never make enough money from these tidbits. He had to find something bigger and better. But what?

One spring morning after Jules had recovered from a bad case of the flu, he went for a walk along one of the boulevards. He was surprised to meet Alexandre Dumas, who had just returned from a trip to the Mediterranean. Neither one mentioned Dumas's money troubles but instead they centered their conversation on writing. Jules brought his friend up to date on what he had written and sold but also told him quite frankly that he desperately needed a job. Dumas listened intently as Jules spoke and said nothing about Jules's appearance. But Dumas was clearly shocked. Jules looked thin and haggard, which was not caused entirely by his bout with influenza. He promised Jules that he would get him a job—and soon. He followed through and several days later Jules became a secretary at the Lyric Theater. Now, at last, he would have a steady salary. When his position seemed secure, he moved into Aristide's apartment building because it was closer to the theater. He became a good secretary and did more than his share of the work. He enjoyed the rehearsals and found that he liked the occasional acting roles he took on. But after six months of working at the theater, Jules saw his early enthusiasm begin to fade away. He soon discovered that theatrical people were less great and glamorous than he had thought. They often had petty arguments over nothing much.

What bothered him most, however, was that the job took up so much of his time, his precious writing and research time. He couldn't go over to the public libraries and read the latest articles on mysterious caves in different parts of the world or look over the reports on what the scientists were finding in them. Was it true they were uncovering fossils dating back millions of years? He also wanted to read more material on the planet Neptune, which was discovered in 1846. Were there more planets beyond Neptune?

In spite of his disillusionment with his job, he stayed with the Lyric Theater for four years. Since it presented only comic operas and operettas and he now had no desire to do this kind of material, he turned instead to trying to write a novel once again. During these years, he wrote

JULES VERNE AT AGE TWENTY-FIVE, PHOTOGRAPHED BY
NADAR. *(Courtesy of the Dublin Library)*

to his father from time to time, but he could tell that Pierre Verne was still unhappy over his choice of careers. Almost every letter from his father told Jules that his destiny was to be a practicing lawyer. One day, after receiving such a letter, Jules sat down and sent back a terse note that said, "I am not coming home. I am going to devote myself to literature. I may become a good writer, but I would never be anything but a poor lawyer."[7]

Mme Verne made his life more bearable by sending him some money and packages of food. She also began to suggest that maybe it was time for him to find a wife—a rich one. He smiled when he read that line, but maybe Mama was right. First, however, he would have to become fairly successful with his writing, and then he could concentrate on searching for a woman who would be happy to be with him for the rest of her life.

At this time, he tried to sell the two novels he had written, but no one seemed interested. He had one rejection after another, and with each one he became more despondent. When would he finally accept that he could not create a story along the lines of Dumas's novels? Maybe he should try one of his adventure stories again. But he was disheartened upon recalling that when he had taken a plot idea over to Monte Cristo one afternoon, he had never had the chance to show it to Dumas.

He decided one morning to take a trip to Dunkirk, on the North Sea. His mother's relatives lived there, and he wrote to them asking if he could stay a week or so. They answered immediately with an invitation to stay even longer. Good! he thought, and knew that sitting by the restless sea would calm his worries about his future. When he had gone there before with his family, he would watch the waves and think about scientists' belief that we all had come from the sea millions of years earlier.

Jules carefully doled out a small amount of money from

his savings and went off on his little vacation. He enjoyed his stay in Dunkirk and returned to Paris in a much more cheerful mood. But his good mood did not last long. When he arrived in the city, he learned that a cholera epidemic was raging, killing many people, and that many theaters had closed, including the Lyric. No one knew for sure when they would all reopen. Once again, Jules was out of a job.

While he wondered what to do next, his mother decided to play matchmaker. She wrote to him that an attractive heiress now living in Nantes would be a good catch. She sent him money for his trip back home, and Jules decided to take her up on the invitation. Perhaps a nice, rich wife would be the answer to all his problems.

He came, he saw, he conquered—almost. Laurence Janmare, the girl he met, was attractive, with a good figure, and seemed impressed that she was dating a young playwright from Paris. All went well until they attended a masquerade ball that summer. It was an extremely hot night, and after the two of them had danced together for a long time, Laurence sat down next to Jules's sister and complained to her about the tightness of her whalebone corset. Jules overheard her and exclaimed, "Could I but fish for whales on those shores!"[8] Everyone heard him, and Laurence's father grabbed his daughter by the arm and practically dragged her outside.

Jules went back to Paris angry and disgusted. Why had he made a remark that sounded like one of the lines from the farces he had written? All of Nantes must be buzzing with gossip about Jules Verne, fortune hunter and rake, a man with no moral values. Those people didn't realize that he had uttered those words because he wanted to sound witty and sophisticated.

From then on, Jules was on guard with what he said and did. His mother tried a few more times to get him interested in rich young women she met, but nothing materialized. In a letter to his mother one day, he told her, "All the delightful young ladies whom I honor with my attentions invariably become engaged to someone else within a fortnight."

All of this ado about nothing brought about excruciating headaches, earaches, and, at times, facial paralysis. During this painful period, he heard from Auguste Lebarge, an old college friend. Auguste wanted Jules to be best man at his wedding in early May in the town of Amiens. Jules told him that he would be honored to do so and would be there a day or two ahead of time. But he had some second thoughts. He wondered if he could see his good friend taking his marriage vows without feeling jealous or envious and resenting his happiness. He somehow knew he could.

7

LOVE AND MARRIAGE

▼

In early May, Jules traveled to Amiens to be best man at Auguste's wedding. When he arrived at the stagecoach inn in the town, he was met by Auguste and his fiancée, Aimée de Viane. In the carriage with them was a young woman in her twenties and her two small daughters. She was introduced to Jules as Honorine Morel, a sister of Aimée's and also a member of the wedding party. Jules was attracted to her from almost the moment they met.

Honorine was pretty and vivacious and had a wonderful sense of humor. The two of them paired off whenever it was possible, but Jules knew he had to find out something very important. Did she have a husband? When he discreetly asked someone that question, he learned that she was a widow and that M. Morel had died a year and a half ago. Jules was elated at the news and stayed in Amiens for an entire week instead of two days.

They went for long walks under the beautiful elm trees in Amiens, and Jules found himself telling Honorine things he had never said to anyone. He told her that he was writing and getting a few articles and poems published but hadn't had any success in doing novels. He also confided

to her that his literary goal in life was to become a successful playwright. Lately, however, he had become interested in science, and he hoped someday to try a novel
with a scientific background. It would take time to develop
his ideas. Honorine was impressed and encouraged him to
work in this category of writing. She approved of his literary ambitions.

The more time he spent with her, the better he liked her.
She sounded as though she'd be happy to marry a man
with his head in the clouds, a dreamer with thoughts he
couldn't even put down on paper. She assured him that
the day would come when he could do that very thing.
She believed in him.

By the end of the week, Jules knew he wanted to marry
Honorine. But how could he when he didn't have a salary?
When he told her this, she suggested that he talk to her
brother, who was a stockbroker and doing very well. Jules
did so and learned that for 50,000 francs he could buy into
a partnership in the stock exchange. Jules knew only one
person who had that kind of money—his father.

He was wise enough not to spring this on Pierre Verne
all at once. He would have to lead up to it with a series of
letters. He did so by dropping a hint here and there, starting with the wonderful time he had had at Auguste's wedding. Then he mentioned meeting Honorine, and how
pretty she was. Later he confessed that she was a widow
with two adorable little girls. Finally he said that he loved
her and wanted to marry her. He could get a position in
the stock exchange if his father could give them 50,000
francs. All of this correspondence took three months. All
along, his father was sending him short notes pointing out
that marrying a young widow with small children would
be a great responsibility. How could he support them?

Jules told him that a job in the stock exchange would
help tremendously. But first he would need 50,000 francs

so that he could buy into a partnership. Pierre Verne wrote back that this was a form of gambling and a risky business. But he gave in eventually and set about finding out some details of Honorine's family. He was pleased with the information and approved of the marriage.

On January 10, 1857, when Jules was twenty-nine years old, he and Honorine were married at the Church of St. Eugène in Paris. About a dozen young people were there in addition to his parents and sisters. Later, all of them went to the wedding breakfast at a modest little restaurant, where Jules added a lighthearted touch to the affair with bright, witty conversation. In accordance with a family tradition, M. Verne read some poetry that he had written for the occasion. He seemed pleased with his son's happiness.

The young couple set up housekeeping near the Bourse—the stock exchange—in a small apartment. It wasn't adequate for a family of four, and several months later, Jules moved his family to better lodgings. He had become very fond of his little stepdaughters, who were two and four years old, and now they would have more room for their toys and games. In addition, the new place gave him a small room where he could shut the door and write.

During the first year of their marriage, Honorine did her best to cater to her husband, especially when he did his writing. She made it a point to awaken him every morning at five with a cup of freshly brewed coffee in her hand. She would then leave him alone at his desk until he had to leave for the office four hours later. During that time she made sure the children played quietly and stayed away from his study.

Even though he was now a businessman, he didn't abandon his writing. He managed to write two scientific articles and another play. But he couldn't sell any of them. Although he then began to turn more of his attention to his job at the Bourse, Jules finally realized that he lacked money sense and could never grasp the workings of this complicated process. The only thing he really enjoyed was the friendship of some of the other brokers who were interested in the arts. He met with them once a week and listened to the stimulating conversations.

One day Aristide paid him a visit and asked if he'd like to go with him on a ship to Scotland. Aristide's brother worked for a steamship company and had offered him two free tickets. Honorine encouraged Jules to go. It would be his first sea voyage; she knew how much he loved the ocean. She also had a feeling that he'd come back with some fresh ideas for his articles and plays. He left at the end of July. Jules was excited and made plans to jot down his impressions of the entire trip in his notebook. He had never been out of France before.

Their ship went to Liverpool, and from there they boarded a train to Scotland. They visited Edinburgh and Glasgow and toured the beautiful lake district. Both of them were impressed with Scotland's rugged mountains covered with purple heather and its bright green moors. Jules wrote letters to Honorine telling her of this country and one time wrote about seeing Edinburgh Castle perched high on a rock looking so majestic and grand.

One of the most thrilling events in their tour was the visit to Fingal's Cave in the Hebrides Islands on the West Coast of Scotland. He recorded his thoughts in his journal:

From this point in the cave, there is an admirable vista broadening out to the open sky, and the water, filled with clear light, allows one to see every detail of the seabed. On the side walls, one sees an astonishing play of light and shadows. When a cloud covers the entrance to the cave, everything grows dark, as when a gauze curtain is dropped over the theatre proscenium. But everything sparkles and glints gaily with the seven colors of the rainbow whenever the sun breaks through again. . . . What an enchanted palace this Fingal's Cave is! Who could be so dull of soul not to believe that it was created by a god for sylphs and water-nymphs![9]

This side trip to the Hebrides and Fingal's Cave filled Jules with romantic and mystical thoughts that wound up leaving an indelible impression on both him and his writings. Images of the place would turn up in several of his later novels, including *Journey to the Center of the Earth* and *The Mysterious Island*. In part thanks to this trip, his future literary efforts would exhibit a special quality that went beyond the scientific aspects.

8

A TASTE OF SUCCESS

▼

When Jules returned home, he was filled with enthusiasm and wrote several short stories and plays. He
once again tried to sell them and couldn't. The only bright
spot in his life at that time was the news that he was going
to become a father. Michel Verne was born on August 3,
1861, and Jules felt proud to have such a fine-looking son.
But now the tiny apartment had five people living there,
and he vowed he'd move soon to a more comfortable
place.

There were times when the baby's crying made it impossible for him to put his thoughts down on paper. Maybe
other writers could create in the midst of bedlam and
noise, but he couldn't. He eventually found himself being
cross with everyone, especially Honorine.

He decided one day to join a new club that consisted of
many kinds of writers, and here he met Félix Tournachon,
better known in Paris as Nadar. The well-known photog-
rapher and man of science was especially interested in
aeronautics and anything to do with flying. Jules didn't realize when they met that Nadar would play an important
role in his life.

When Michel was a few months old, a news item in a Paris newspaper caught Jules's attention. A man named Nadar was asking for subscriptions to construct the biggest balloon that had ever been built. This article excited Jules because Nadar was an acquaintance of his and he admired his thoughts and ideas, but there was another reason. Jules had been interested in passenger balloons ever since reading a short story by Edgar Allan Poe called "A Balloon Hoax," about a news dispatch that told about the successful flight of a passenger balloon crossing the Atlantic in only three days. He was also impressed by an 1835 short story by Poe called "The Unparalleled Adventure of Hans Pfaal," about a Dutchman who flew to the moon in a balloon filled with a secret gas.

At that time many people in France were reading Poe's poems and eerie tales. They seemed to enjoy letting themselves get scared to death. His writing was so real that when people read his stories they believed they could hear the pounding of a dead man's heart or the frantic screams of a man being buried alive. Jules read them all. He also liked the American author's stories about secret codes and buried treasure, especially "The Gold Bug," in which Captain Kidd's code was cracked. Later on, Poe's short story "Three Sundays in a Week" made an impression on Jules and helped him in writing his most successful novel, *Around the World in Eighty Days.*

Poe's balloon stories were on Jules's mind as he read and reread the newspaper article about Nadar. He had to admit to himself that the stories didn't have much scientific basis, but they showed that people were becoming increasingly interested in this kind of travel. Maybe he could work with Nadar on his gigantic balloon called *The Giant,* and quite possibly the huge passenger balloon could become the magic carpet of the future. He made up his mind to pay a visit to his friend as soon as possible.

But when he visited Nadar a few days later, he was surprised to learn that this talented man didn't believe that the balloon could really succeed as a means of transportation. He bluntly told Jules that the only reason he was building *The Giant* was for the money and the publicity it would bring him so that he could construct a primitive kind of helicopter. Eventually that would lead to other flying machines, which were what he really cared about.

Jules went home that afternoon not believing what he had heard. How could Nadar keep saying over and over that the passenger balloon had no chance of materializing and that too many things could happen? Not true, Jules thought. I'll show him that he is wrong, and I'll do it by writing a book describing all of the details I've discovered through my years of research.

Jules had been interested in aerial navigation for a long time and was constantly reading the latest scientific manuals on the subject. Armed with many details, he sat down one morning at his desk and jotted down some thoughts about balloons that had been swirling around in his head for days. Why couldn't someone take two balloons of unequal size and place the smaller one within the larger? The inner balloon, filled with air, could maintain the outer bag. Why couldn't the two bags be connected with a valve to permit circulation of the hydrogen gas? The gas from the outer balloon would then flow into the inner balloon instead of escaping into the atmosphere. The dimension of the outer bag would decrease, and the balloon would be able to descend without losing any gas. It seemed possible to keep a balloon afloat for a long time.

The more Jules thought about his theory, the more excited he became. He wrote down some of his ideas while they were still fresh in his mind, and when he had done so, he went back to material he was writing on Africa. He'd been interested in this country for many years and in his research had turned up intriguing facts and places he longed to explore.

One morning, Jules happened to read in the newspaper about an international race going on to discover the source of the Nile, the longest river in the world. Africa was an unknown area of the world to Europeans at this time, and it stirred people's imaginations. Several explorers had managed to reach the unknown territory between the Nile and Lake Chad. Was the source there? Jules suddenly had a brilliant idea. His balloon would carry the explorers who would find the place where the Nile began!

While Nadar worked on *The Giant* and equipped it with double-decker bunks, a kitchen, and a darkroom, Jules began writing his book *Five Weeks in a Balloon*. Honorine didn't see him except at mealtimes, when he sat at the table for ten or fifteen minutes before he went back to his writing. Later, in May 1862, Honorine wrote Jules's mother: "Have you had strawberries at Chantenay yet? Jules is eating some now as he finishes a story about balloons. There are manuscripts everywhere—nothing but manuscripts! Let's hope they don't finish up under the cooking pot!"[10]

As Jules worked on his book, he combined his extensive knowledge of Africa with that of balloons. His book eventually became a nonfiction account of what it would be like to travel in a passenger balloon and discover the source of the Nile. He pointed out that the travelers wouldn't get malaria from the steamy jungles below or have to worry about attacks from ferocious animals or run from witch doctors ready to torture them or eat them.

When he finished the manuscript, he sent it to a publisher. It came back. He sent it out again. It came back. During that year he had many rejections. When it came back on the fifteenth try, that did it. He took the pages and threw them into the fireplace. Honorine happened to walk into the room at that moment and, when she realized what he was doing, let out a scream and rushed over to rescue the material. She hid the book for more than a week and gave it to him only after he promised he'd never do that again.

Disheartened, Jules wrote his father:

It is as if the moment I get an idea or launch any literary project, the idea or the project at once goes wrong. If I write a play for a particular theater director, he moves elsewhere; if I think of a good title, three days later I see it on the billboards announcing someone else's play; if I write an article, another appears on the same subject. Even if I discovered a new planet, I believe it would at once explode, just to prove me wrong.[11]

One day, in great desperation, he paid a visit to his old friend Alexandre Dumas and asked him to read the material. Dumas liked it and said that it had possibilities. He sent Jules to a novelist named Brehat, who told him to go see a publisher named Hetzel.

Jules wasted little time in going to Pierre Hetzel's office on the Rue Jacob. Jules and the publisher hit it off from the moment they met. Hetzel told him that he had special interest in children's books and was now publishing a juvenile magazine. Perhaps Jules could supply some stories for both. When he leafed through the pages of *Five Weeks in a Balloon,* he nodded from time to time, but when he handed it back to the nervous author, he shook his head. No, he couldn't use it the way it was written. But he told Jules to rewrite it as an adventure story based on scientific facts and to come back in two weeks.

As Jules went to the door, Hetzel said he had the makings of a great storyteller. This bit of encouragement lit a fire under him, and he could hardly wait to get home to make the changes. He knew he could do it.

And he did. The words seemed to flow, and he had no trouble creating three adventurous characters: Dr. Samuel Ferguson, an English explorer; Joe Wilson, a faithful servant; and the third, Dick Kennedy, a courageous Scotsman. He placed them in the *Victoria,* a passenger balloon scheduled to go across Africa from east to west following the trade winds. The highly intelligent Dr. Ferguson had already figured out how to ascend and descend to catch the favorable air currents. He had equipped his balloon with a special furnace that permitted him to control the temperature of the hydrogen gas inside the balloon bag. By heating the gas, causing the gas to expand, the *Victoria* could rise. By allowing the gas to cool again, he could make it go down.

Jules enjoyed maneuvering the *Victoria* over the jungles of Africa, where the local inhabitants thought she was a foreign god. One time he moored her on the top of a breadfruit tree so that she would be safe from attack by some of the people below. On another occasion, her trail rope became entangled in the tusks of an elephant that began to race wildly over the terrain with the balloon in tow. He couldn't resist putting her in the midst of a blinding rainstorm and had Dr. Ferguson battle to make her rise high above the clouds and away from the flashes of lightning. At the end of the story, after many more life-threatening experiences, the three men finish the journey without the cabin, clinging to the net of the sinking balloon.

The novel opens with a brief factual account of African exploration up to that time, and then the reader is promised:

Africa is about to yield the secret of its vast solitude at last. A modern Odysseus will find the key to the

problem which the learned of sixteen centuries have
not been able to solve. Formerly, to seek the sources
of the Nile was regarded as the act of a madman; a
wild dream, in fact.

Dr. Ferguson is Verne's modern Odysseus. The original
Odysseus, or Ulysses, was the hero of Homer's *Odyssey*,
the ancient Greek epic. Dr. Ferguson, along with his two
companions, reaches Lake Victoria, considered by real explorers to be the source of the Nile. Dick Kennedy tells
them their discoveries are entirely in accord with the scientific predictions.

Two weeks later, Jules returned to Hetzel with his revised
manuscript. After making one small change, the publisher
accepted it and gave him a long-term contract; Jules would
provide three volumes a year for 1,925 francs per book.
Jules went home in a daze. It had finally happened! Now
he could live off his writings and not waste time doing jobs
that gave him money but had nothing to do with further-
ing his creative abilities.

Five Weeks in a Balloon came out in January, 1863, and
was an immediate best-seller among adults and children.
The *Victoria*, in spite of its heart-thumping moments, had
enjoyed a successful flight. On the other hand, Nadar's balloon, *The Giant*, had crashed in Hanover, Germany, nearly
killing the adventurer and his wife.

9

IMAGINARY VOYAGES

▼

The success of *Five Weeks in a Balloon* announced to the world that a new kind of book had arrived: the science fiction novel. Within a year, nearly everyone in France recognized the name of Jules Verne as one of the important French novelists. This book was the first of his stories that he called voyages. They would occupy him for the next forty years. He was now thirty-five years old. He would always remember that the year 1863 was a turning point in his life.

With the recognition came some money, and Jules could afford to move his family into an attracive house in the suburbs. Now Honorine could entertain their friends with dinner parties, and Jules could enjoy some interesting discussions with guests well versed in literature and science. But what he liked the most was the large study where he could close the door and write undisturbed for hours. He wrote his first drafts in pencil and then in pen. When his material came back from the printer, he usually went over it seven or eight times to make sure all of it was correct.

He enjoyed working with Hetzel, his publisher, and the

A CARTOON OF JULES VERNE ENTITLED "VERNE, THE
WONDERFUL."

two men became good friends. At this time, Hetzel became the owner of a juvenile magazine that combined education and recreation, and he believed that Jules's writings would appeal to the magazine's young readers. He made plans to run Jules's stories serially before they came out in book form, and in the spring of 1864, the first installment of *The Adventures of Captain Hatteras* made its appearance.

In it, the hero goes on a perilous journey to explore the unknown lands of the Arctic. This novel is remarkable for the information it contained. A famous French explorer named Charcot stated that Jules's description of life on board ship was authentic down to the smallest detail.

Jules found his research about the frozen North utterly fascinating and longed to be in Captain Hatteras's shoes. He pored over maps, read accounts of its climate and plants and animals, and studied all of the eyewitness accounts he could find. Once again he created three characters: Hatteras, an English multimillionaire obsessed with the idea of becoming the first man to reach the North Pole; Captain Altamont, an American and a rival explorer; and Dr. Clawbonny, a scholarly doctor.

Once again, the three adventurers encounter one harrowing experience after another, including menacing icebergs; ferocious polar bears; wild, howling snowstorms; and bitterly cold weather. But Captain Hatteras is a leader and is determined to reach the North Pole in spite of any setbacks. At the end of the journey, he loses his mind.

Even though Jules was wrong about some of the details of the region, the general impression was so real that Admiral Richard E. Byrd, who explored the continent of Antarctica, said in his book *Alone,* "It is Jules Verne who guides me." Other explorers who read his novel were also influenced by his knowledge of the Arctic and how he made it possible for Captain Hatteras finally to reach his goal.

In the summer of 1864, Jules took his family to his parents' place in Chantenay. His brother and three sisters were also married by now and had brought their small children. Jules's mother, a very wise woman, gave Jules a small room where he could do his thinking and writing.

Several times when his family gathered around the dining room table to talk and reminisce, Jules would slip away to work on his next novel. He had recently met with the noted geographer Charles Saint-Claire Deville and discussed volcanoes with him. Deville had explored them all over the world and had recently descended into the crater of Stromboli in the Mediterranean Sea when it lay dormant for a while.

Deville believed that hundreds of active volcanoes and thousands of dormant ones were once distributed over the earth's surface. It was possible that they were connected by deep underground tunnels. If this were true, mightn't it be possible to travel from the crater of an extinct volcano to the earth's interior?

When Jules went home that evening, his head was filled with thoughts of an imaginary journey to the center of the earth. His hero would be a mineralogist by the name of Lidenbrock, a professor from Hamburg, Germany, who discovers a coded message on the back of an ancient Icelandic book. After much hard work, the professor figures out that the words were written by a sixteenth-century alchemist well known for his intelligence. Lidenbrock tries to decode the material but winds up with weird words, such as:

sgtssmf
oseido
esruel
rrilsa

nicdrke
kediil

Eventually, the professor and the nephew use their knowledge of Latin to find the key and are dumbfounded when they realize they must read the message from right to left. When they do so, they discover that the learned alchemist believed it possible to reach the center of the earth through the crater of an extinct Icelandic volcano, the Snoffels. The professor persuades Axel, his nephew, and Hans, an Icelandic tour guide, to go with him on this expedition. Axel is reluctant to go because he is in love with a beautiful girl he plans to marry soon, but he finally agrees to accompany Lidenbrock.

The three explorers set out with all kinds of food and equipment. Each one carries a lantern powered by a kind of electricity invented by Jules but based on the work of a German physicist living in Paris at the time.

Holding their lanterns in front of them, they descend into the extinct volcano and follow a labyrinth of tunnels that leads into the earth's interior. On the forty-eighth day they reach a mammoth cavern whose floor is covered with a large and awesome sea: "A vast limitless expanse of water . . . spread before us, until it was lost in the distance. . . . It was in reality an ocean, with all the characteristics of an inland sea, only horribly wild—so rigid, cold, and savage."

To explore the underground sea, the three men build a raft, and their adventures begin. They pass a boiling volcanic island that could erupt at any moment. They sail past a forest of mushrooms more than forty feet high. They stare at terrible battles of prehistoric monsters who fight each other to the death. They see the flora and fauna that belong to a world millions of years ago. What astounds them most of all is a glimpse of a humanlike creature older than history. But is this creature really a man? He is about twelve feet tall and has a mane of long, wild hair and a head as large as that of a buffalo. (Could this be the ancestor of the Abominable Snowman?) The men aren't too sure what they are seeing because they are in a weird kind of light that makes them feel they are in a fantasy land.

At one place in the novel, Verne added a suspenseful episode by having Axel take a wrong turn as he follows his uncle and the guide through the long tunnel. Axel tries his best for several hours to find the passageway where the three of them had met, but it has vanished; now there is only a wall of solid rock. Axel knows he faces death from lack of food and water and says:

In the midst of all these horrible sources of anguish and despair, a new horror took possession of my soul. My lamp, by falling down, had got out of order. I had no means of repairing it. Its light was already becoming paler and paler, and it would soon expire!

At the end of the story, the explorers use their remaining stick of dynamite to clear a tunnel and the explosion starts an earthquake. They are flung up through the crater of a volcano to Stromboli Island in the Mediterranean, where it is sunny and beautiful. Eventually, they get back to Hamburg.

Jules's knowledge of evolution and geology overwhelmed his readers. How did he know so much? They were also impressed by his eagerness to share with them any of the latest news from the science field that he obtained from detailed journals or reputable scientists who were his friends. People interested in archaeology and paleontology practically stood in line to grab copies of *A Journey to the Center of the Earth* when it came out in

1864. They wanted to read for themselves an item they had heard about.

In this book, Jules had the professor discover fossil remains and a human skull in a section of the cavern. Until that time, most fossil remains had been found in bogs, marshes, and swamps, but Jules was almost sure that they could also be found in caves. A few years after the publication of *A Journey to the Center of the Earth*, prehistoric remains of men, women, and children were found in caves in Spain and France.

☞ 10 ☜

A Trip to the Moon

▼

The reading public wondered what Jules Verne would write about next. Hetzel, his publisher, wondered, too, and when he heard he was amazed—and delighted. Jules announced that he planned to take his readers to the moon. Hetzel realized that Jules was truly on his way to writing the literature of the future.

Ever since Jules had read Edgar Allan Poe's short story about going to the moon in a balloon, he had been fascinated with man's attempts to get there. He had read earlier stories, too, including one written by a Greek named Lucian that told about a ship sailing to the edge of the world, where a huge water spout lifted it to the moon. He enjoyed reading "The Man in the Moon" by Francis Godwin, an English bishop, whose hero traveled to the moon on an open platform pulled by trained swans. But the story that really impressed him was written by a famous French writer named Cyrano de Bergerac in the seventeenth century. In this story, a passenger travels to the moon in a wooden machine powered by exploding firecrackers. Jules felt that a more sophisticated version of this device could actually get a human being to the moon.

He began to read everything he could find on space, planets, telescopes, weather, meteors, and gunpowder and used close to five hundred references in his search for details. He also thumbed through some of the recent novels describing trips to the moon and to Venus and Mars. But although they were entertaining, they weren't based on any scientific facts. Jules's book would be entertaining *and* scientific. As he delved into his research, he acknowledged to himself that he would need some advice in mathematics and that it was time once again to confer with his cousin Henri.

When they met, Henri listened patiently as an excited Jules filled him in on his new imaginary voyage. Jules told him that he had been following closely the Civil War in America and had been impressed with the technical advances made by both sides in their use of artillery. As an ardent pacifist, he wondered what could be done with these powerful weapons of destruction when the war was over. He confided to Henri that he had dashed off a satire in which he had suggested that these weapons be used to bombard the moon. It was a crazy idea, of course, but the more he thought about it, the more he could see it actually happening.

Jules went on and said that he planned to set his story in America and center it around the Gun Club of Baltimore, which consisted of retired artillery men who had fought in the Civil War. Most of them were missing an arm or a leg and had become bored with their humdrum lives. They wanted something exciting to do. When their president, Impey Barbicane, suggests that they try to shoot a projectile to the moon, they respond with great enthusiasm. They can hardly wait to get the plan under way.

Henri, more practical than Jules, made sure that his cousin went over his calculations very carefully. What muzzle velocity did the projectile need to escape the grav-

BARBICANE TAKES THE FLOOR AND TALKS TO MEMBERS OF
THE GUN CLUB, IN A SCENE FROM *FROM THE EARTH TO THE
MOON*. (Courtesy of the Library of Congress)

itational pull of the earth? Jules answered that from his own intensive research he had learned that any object leaving the earth at a velocity of seven miles per second would escape the earth's gravitational pull and continue moving into space. His projectile, made of aluminum and shaped like a huge bullet, would be fired from a monstrous cannon in a desolate part of Florida and head straight for the moon.

When they met again, Jules had his whole plot and storyline set up and told his cousin that he had decided to place a man in the bullet or shell and make him the first human being in space. He also said that the site chosen by the members of the Gun Club would be at Stone Hill near Tampa, Florida. There would be three characters: Barbicane, the club president; Nicholl, a gunnery expert; and a Frenchman named Michel Ardan who had volunteered to be placed in the projectile even before the Americans had signed up. And there would be two dogs, Diana and Satellite, who would cross-breed with dogs on the moon. They would complete their journey in ninety-seven hours, thirteen minutes, and twenty seconds, when the moon would then be full.

Henri couldn't help nodding his approval of Jules's new and crazy adventure but gave him advice to make sure his astronauts wouldn't perish abruptly. Jules listened intently and finally agreed to follow some of Henri's suggestions. To make his cousin happy, he redesigned the shell as a spacecraft with padded walls and equipped it with a chemical device that produced a steady supply of oxygen. He had his passengers take along an ample supply of water and concentrated food as well as a variety of scientific instruments, tools, and weapons. He also gave them maps of the moon and seeds for planting when they arrived. Finally, he attached several small rockets to the outside of the projectile that would slow the descent of the men.

In Jules's book *From the Earth to the Moon,* when the day for the launching arrives, five million people from all over the world gather at Stone Hill. The huge cannon, named the Columbiad, is loaded with charges of gun cotton, a kind of gunpowder. The projectile is lifted into the air and lowered into the mouth of the cannon. Finally, the astronauts synchronize their watches, wave to the cheering crowd, and enter their compartment from an underground tunnel. The scaffolding is removed from around the mouth of the cannon. There is a deathlike stillness everywhere. All eyes are turned in one direction.

Murphy, the timekeeper, begins his count, starting with one and going up instead of down. "Thirty-five! Thirty-six! Thirty-seven! Thirty-eight! Thirty-nine! FIRE!"

Touching a button, Murphy closes the connection and sends an electric current into the heart of the cannon. "The unearthly, ear-piercing, drum-rending, brain-shattering roar which follows his words we must not attempt to describe," says the book's narrator.

The concussion causes earthquakes throughout Florida, tidal waves far out to sea, and a disturbance in the atmosphere which covers the sky for eleven days. Eventually, the giant telescope set up on a Colorado mountain spots the projectile, but something is wrong, terribly wrong. Instead of landing *on* the moon, the projectile has been swept into orbit *around* the moon. It has become an artificial satellite. The story ends here with a promise from the author that a sequel would follow. He kept his word, but *Around the Moon* appeared five years later, a long time for his readers to wait before hearing if the three men had survived.

In this book Jules explains what happened. Just as his astronauts were about to land on the moon, the spacecraft almost collided with a meteoroid. Its gravitational pull threw them off course, and they were swept into the

AN ARTIST'S DEPICTION OF THE CANNON IN *FROM THE EARTH TO THE MOON*. (Courtesy of the Library of Congress)

AN ARTIST'S RENDITION OF THE ROCKET IN *FROM THE EARTH TO THE MOON* AND ITS SEQUEL, *AROUND THE MOON*.

moon's lunar orbit. In the sequel, the astronauts, after circling the moon many times, fire their rockets so they can get out of the orbit and land on the lunar surface, but something else goes wrong and they find themselves falling into the Pacific Ocean. They are rescued by sailors from a nearby American ship and later are hailed as heroes by the entire country.

While the two novels had a number of errors in the science, critics praised Jules Verne for his gift of prophecy: the location of the launch site, the shape of the capsule, the weightlessness of space, the use of rockets to alter the orbit, and the splashdown at sea. More recently, Frank Borman, an astronaut on the *Apollo 8* mission in 1968 and an admirer of Verne's books, wrote a letter to Jules's grandson, a professional writer, and said, "Our space vehicle was launched from Florida, like Barbicane's; it had the same weight and the same height, and it splashed down in the Pacific a mere two and a half miles from the point mentioned in the novel."[12]

Borman also remembered that when his wife read *From the Earth to the Moon*, she was terrified that he might never come back. He suggested that she read the sequel. She wasn't the only one who found the stories realistic. Many of Verne's readers believed that he was writing about a spaceship that actually existed and that a trip to the moon was indeed being planned. Hundreds of them wrote to Jules begging him to take them along on this fantastic voyage. He was overwhelmed by their reaction to his two books, and in a note to Paul, he said: "The Parisians are certainly brave. Some of them are determined by hook or crook to embark on my projectile."

☞ 11 ☜

THE COTTAGE ON THE BAY

▼

By the time Jules Verne was thirty-seven years old, his books were being read around the world. Some of the translations may have been garbled, but young and old alike were caught up in his thrilling tales of adventure. But at home, Honorine realized that she had to make her husband slow down. She didn't approve of his writing two books at one time, which he did fairly often and was now doing again. She never dreamed that he had a third on his mind.

He had begun work on *The Children of Captain Grant*, which featured two teenagers, Mary and Robert, traveling to many countries to find their missing father. A century later, Walt Disney used this novel as a basis for his movie *In Search of the Castaways*. Jules enjoyed writing this story because it involved a desert island, and he spent many hours working on the details. But when his publisher, Hetzel, asked him to finish a geography of France because its elderly writer had become very ill, Jules barely hesitated before accepting the job. He needed the extra money. He was learning that lavish entertaining was expensive, and the bills were piling up. In a letter to his father he wrote:

I am working like a galley slave on an "Illustrated Geography of France." Théophile Lavalée is dying; and I have taken over. . . . I hope at the same time to write the first volume of "Under the Oceans," the outline of which is completely finished and which will really be marvelous.[13]

The outline to which Jules referred would later become *Twenty Thousand Leagues Under the Sea.*

His adventure tale concerning Captain Grant centered around a worldwide search for the captain, whose ship was wrecked somewhere along the thirty-seventh parallel. His two children, Mary and Robert, sail on a yacht, the *Duncan,* owned by Lord Glenarvan and his wife, who are friends of the family. When they reach an island off the cost of Scotland, the crew catches a shark whose stomach contains a champagne bottle with a message written in English, French, and German. Many of the words are illegible from the seawater seeping in, but Glenarvan figures out that the message was sent from the *Brittania,* a three-masted schooner under Grant's command. It says that Grant and two of his men are being held prisoner by Indians in Patagonia at the tip of South America.

Lord Glenarvan, his wife, Mary, Robert, and the crew of the *Duncan* set out to find Grant and travel to South America, Australia, and New Zealand but finally and regretfully have to turn back. Captain Grant doesn't seem to be anywhere. But when they stop at Marie-Theresa Island in the Pacific, Mary and Robert hear a voice in the night shouting for help. They are sure it is their father. The others on board the yacht believe that the children are having a hallucination and don't check it out until the next morning. It is not an illusion. The three men are found in fairly good shape, and the Grant children are reunited with their fa-

TRAVELING BY GIANT CONDOR IN *THE CHILDREN OF
CAPTAIN GRANT.*

ther after a search that has taken them across several continents and oceans.

Jules's hectic schedule at this time brought about sleepless nights, severe headaches, and a return of his facial paralysis. He finally admitted to Honorine that he needed a vacation. He rented a summer cottage for the family at Le Crotoy, a fishing village on the northern coast of France where he had spent a few days the year before. He had learned a long time ago that the sea always had a calming effect on him. He was sure it would perform its magic again.

During those summer months, he fell in love with the little house on the bay on the Somme River. The area was wild and desolate, with sand dunes everywhere and only the plaintive cry of the sea gulls breaking the stillness from time to time. He especially liked to watch the rising tide coming in and the shrimp boats returning with the catch of the day. Jules was content with the isolation. Five-year-old Michel tagged along with him wherever he went and also found many things to do on his own. Honorine and the girls decided that this was not the life for them and went often to Amiens to visit relatives.

Jules set up a schedule for his writing and had the discipline to follow it. He would rise at dawn, watch the fishing fleet sail off, and listen to the slap, slap, slap of the waves hitting the beach. It was music to his ears. He would work until noon, have lunch, then go for a long walk across the dunes behind his house enjoying the stiff wind stinging his face. At least once a week he would go into the village itself and stare at something in the town square. That something was three cannonballs secured by chains.

This was all that remained of the historic day in the fifteenth century when Joan of Arc was brought to Crotoy as a prisoner. Without a doubt, Jules must have stood there thinking back to times when the little peasant girl heard voices from Heaven telling her she must lead French troops in battle to save her country. She did that and defeated the English five times but eventually was declared a witch and burned at the stake.

One afternoon when Jules walked past the dock in the village, he saw a fishing smack up for sale. It was a weatherbeaten old vessel with broad sails and an open hull. It appealed to him, and later that day it belonged to him. He immediately looked for an experienced carpenter who gave the open hull a forecastle big enough for two crew members and a cabin suitable for Jules and a friend or two. He furnished it with narrow wooden benches topped by seaweed mattresses and named it *Saint Michel*, after his son. He scurried around for two able seamen for his part-time crew and found two retired sailors who had spent their lives at sea. Michel was particularly mesmerized by one of the sailors, Alfred Berlot, who had sailed the seven seas and who had once been captured by cannibals. Michel had to hear the story many times, especially the part when he was about to be eaten but escaped just in time.

When Jules was aboard his boat, he was able to relax completely. He eventually made the cabin into a small study and spent many hours creating his stories there. For a change of pace, he would dress in rough seaman's clothing and take his turn at the tiller. He felt alive and exhilarated whenever he did so with the wind whipping across his face and the salty sea spray stinging his lips.

Throughout the summer and fall of 1866, he put the finishing touches to *The Children of Captain Grant* and the geography book of France for Hetzel. During this period he wrote his father: "This extra work will give Honorine the few thousand francs she needs for the house and to keep herself decently dressed and it will allow me to make a crossing with Paul on the 'Great Eastern' which, as you know, I have been wanting to do for a long time."

Late in 1866, Jules turned over the two manuscripts to Hetzel and contacted his brother Paul to see if he was interested in going on a cruise on the *Great Eastern* to America. Paul had recently resigned from the navy and was now working as a stockbroker in Paris. This trip had been on Jules's mind ever since the time he and Aristide had seen the ship being built near London a few years earlier.

He was pleased when his brother agreed, Paul said to choose a date so they could make plans. Jules had a special reason for going: A sea story was forming in his mind, one that made it necessary to be in the midst of a great ocean where he could peer down into the murky depths. He somehow knew that this imaginary journey would be spectacular and would become his masterpiece.

12

ON TO AMERICA

▼

Jules and his brother, Paul, lined up a cruise to America on the *Great Eastern* for March 23, 1867. When the time came, they traveled to England to get aboard the great ship at Liverpool, and when they were on board, Jules made sure to inspect everything that wasn't off-limits. He was amazed when he saw that the powerful paddle wheels were fifty feet across and as high as some apartment buildings. He was impressed by the elegant, mirrored ballroom and staterooms and the interesting passengers he met at dinner.

Jules made it a point to search for one special traveler: Cyrus Field, who was responsible for laying the Atlantic Cable. When he found him, the two men had an enjoyable conversation, and Jules asked many pertinent questions and stashed away the answers for his new novel. He also managed to talk to some of the seamen who had worked on the cable and heard hair-raising accounts of the "monsters" they saw down at the bottom of the sea. He was all ears when they told him about the giant squid that had become entangled in the cable lines. Once again he filed the story away in his memory.

JULES SAW THE *GREAT EASTERN* BEING BUILT AND PROMISED
HIMSELF THAT ONE DAY HE WOULD BE ONE OF HER
PASSENGERS. *(Courtesy of the United States Navy)*

As for staring down into the murky depths of the ocean,
Jules had little opportunity. Several violent storms en-
gulfed them on their trip, and in his journal he wrote: "The
'Great Eastern,' in spite of its size, was tossed about like a
cork, its bow was swept clean away—it was terrifying. . . .
Ah, the sea! What an admirable element it is!"[14]

During one storm he staggered to a railing, held on for
dear life, and stared down into the angry, churning water.
What was down there? Monsters never seen before? Giant
slithering snakes? Man-eating fish or plants? Squids bigger
than the one caught in the Atlantic Cable? Standing there,

he soaked up enough atmosphere to at least begin his new story in his imagination.

When Jules and Paul landed in New York City, they stayed at a Fifth Avenue hotel, had dinner at the famous Delmonico's Restaurant, and strolled along Broadway in the evening. They saw a play at the Barnum Theater called *The French Consul* and took a train to upper New York State to see Niagara Falls. The trip took them through the Mohawk Valley, the setting of James Fenimore Cooper's Leatherstocking Tales, which they had read as boys. They were so thrilled that they called each other Hawkeye and Chingachgook, two of Cooper's main characters, for the rest of the day.

They were both enchanted with the awesome and majestic beauty of the falls, and Jules later used them in two of his books, *Family Without a Name* and *The Master of the World*. Jules wished they could stay an extra day or two, but he knew it wasn't possible. In his journal he wrote of "Niagara Falls, where the roar of the water, the spray, the sunlight playing on the vapors, and the excitement and the briny tang of the cataract hold you in perpetual ecstasy."

Jules and Paul left America reluctantly. They wanted to see more of this young and vibrant republic. Jules later wrote an article for a magazine, *The Youth's Companion*, in which he said, "I'm ashamed to admit that I spent only a week in your country. But it couldn't be helped; my round trip ticket did not allow a longer stay."

When Jules came home, he put his numerous notes on the ship aside; he would later incorporate them into a novel called *The Floating City*. But right now he had to sit down and work on his story about the sea, the restless, ever-changing sea. He was about to take his readers to a fascinating place where they had never been before.

He made many trips to the Archives of the National Library in Paris, where he researched everything he could

JULES WAS SO IMPRESSED WITH THIS VIEW OF
NIAGARA FALLS THAT HE USED
THE FALLS IN SEVERAL OF HIS LATER NOVELS.
(Courtesy of the Library of Congress)

find on underwater exploration. He spent many hours researching the history of submersibles. His characters would be placed in a submarine—a super-special one that people would talk about for a long time.

He read with great interest the accounts of the early attempts to travel under water. He was amused by the legend that in 333 B.C. Alexander the Great dived beneath the Aegean Sea in a glass barrel through which he saw whales and all kinds of denizens of the deep. Could it be true? He was also amused by the story of Cornelius van Drebbel, a Dutchman who in 1620 built a submersible rowing boat with an air-purification system. The boat, covered with greased hides, was demonstrated on the Thames River near London and was described as "an invisible eel." Jules paid some attention to David Bushnell's 1775 invention, the first genuine submarine. This American's boat, the *Turtle*, was used in 1776 to attack a British flagship blockading New York Harbor. But what really caught his attention was the practical hand-powered submarine invented by the American Robert Fulton in 1800. It had been called the *Nautilus*.

The boat created by Fulton was cigar-shaped with a watertight hull twenty feet long and six feet wide. Three men operated the craft in such a way that it could make a six-hour dive. It held great promise for the future. Jules was fortunate enough to come across an article by Fulton in the library in Paris. It contained many details of the invention. Jules made many notes and made sure to jot down a remark made by the inventor: He planned to use his submarine to destroy the navies of the world and to abolish war forever. Aha! Jules thought. I'll be able to use this in my novel somewhere.

After doing more research on oceanography, diving apparatuses, and the latest inventions used in exploring under the sea, Jules headed for his beloved *Saint Michel*. Loaded down with reference material, he made himself comfortable in his tiny floating study and began to write. He propped Victor Hugo's novel *Toilers of the Sea* up against the lamp for inspiration. This dramatic story, combining romance and adventure on a steamboat, had recently been published and was selling well. Before long, Jules was caught up in the novel and disappeared from the everyday world.

Once again, Jules used three main characters and placed them in a fantastic submarine commanded by the brilliant but slightly mad Captain Nemo. The three men were Professor Pierre Aronnax, a famous French biologist; Conseil, a manservant; and Ned Land, a Canadian harpooner. The professor acts as the narrator of what happens to the three of them.

Jules opens his novel with details of what is going on at sea in the year 1866. Something strange and terrible is happening. A number of ships have been rammed and almost sunk by a mysterious object. What is it? Could it be Moby Dick, the famous white whale? Could it be an immense kraken, that legendary sea monster whose tentacles can envelop a huge ship and pull it down to the bottom of the ocean floor? Or is it the enormous sea serpent everyone is talking about these days? All of these theories were being discussed in many countries, and certain leaders decide that something has to be done—and soon.

A ship equipped by the United States government is sent out to track down this elusive "monster." The French professor is invited to join the expedition along with Conseil and Ned Land. After some harrowing experiences as they seek out the object, they get too close when they give chase in one area, and the frigate is sunk. The three men escape with their lives but find themselves taken on board a unique submarine, which turns out to be the mysterious "creature" raising havoc in the Atlantic Ocean.

They soon learn that they are actually prisoners of Captain Nemo, who tells them that they will be on board the *Nautilus* for the rest of their lives. He could never allow them to return to the outside world and reveal what they have seen and heard. The three captives only stare at him in disbelief. Who is this man? Outwardly, he is tall, dark-haired, with piercing black eyes, and has a melancholy look about him. He tells them that he hates any kind of tyranny and will prowl the seas seeking vengeance for those who have been destroyed by rulers with unlimited power. The professor realizes that this man must have a terrible secret in his life that is making him act this way.

Later the captain takes his prisoners on a guided tour of his submarine. It is a luxury vessel containing a library with twelve thousand books, an art gallery, a marine museum, a spectacular organ, and an immense drawing room filled with priceless paintings and tapestries. It has sliding wall panels that open to reveal wide picture windows. The men can look out into the ocean and see hundreds of different kinds of fish and sea animals as if they were at an aquarium.

When the three men have dinner with Captain Nemo, they find the food quite different—tasty but puzzling. Their host tells them that everything they are eating has come from the sea and that a menu would read:

Turtle fillet
Liver of dolphin
A cream dessert made from whale's milk
Preserves of anemone (a tiny sea animal)

The captives are made fairly comfortable as they travel along in the *Nautilus* and experience all kinds of adventures. During the ten months of their imprisonment they get the opportunity to don diving suits and go on a hunt at the bottom of the sea, where they kill their prey in-

A SCENE FROM *TWENTY THOUSAND LEAGUES UNDER THE SEA* IN WHICH CAPTAIN NEMO MEASURES THE HEIGHT OF THE SUN. *(Courtesy of the Library of Congress)*

IN THIS SCENE FROM *TWENTY THOUSAND LEAGUES UNDER THE SEA*, THE THREE PRISONERS AND THE SEA CREATURES STARE AT ONE ANOTHER. *(Courtesy of the Library of Congress)*

stantly with glass bullets fired from an air gun. They take part in destroying a huge school of devilfish that enmeshes the boat with their tentacles. They visit a fishery where they see a mollusk that has in its jaws a pearl weighing close to five hundred pounds.

On their long trip around the world, they also encounter an underwater forest, the lost continent of Atlantis, fabulous treasures from sunken ships, terrifying sea creatures, and even the South Pole. And always they have marine life staring in at them, such as killer sharks, menacing octopuses, and mammoth sea spiders. Electric lights from the submarine make the creatures visible at all times.

Their interesting voyage comes to an abrupt halt one day when they meet up with a man-of-war ship. Captain Nemo doesn't hesitate for a moment. He orders it destroyed, showing no mercy for the hundreds of sailors who drown right in front of their eyes. The prisoners are horrified, but the professor has second thoughts when he sees Captain Nemo enter his room soon after and kneel down before a portrait of a young woman and two small children. He can hear him sobbing and knows his deed has given him anguish. Professor Aronnax realizes that the man can't be all bad.

At the end of the novel, after traveling twenty thousand leagues—sixty thousand miles—under the sea, the unexpected happens. Nemo, his crew, his boat, and the prisoners are swept into the notorious Maelstrom off the Lofoten Islands near Norway. The three men survive this deadly whirlpool and wonder if the captain has been as lucky. The professor hopes so and says:

> I also hope that his powerful vessel has conquered the sea at its most terrible gulf, and that the "Nautilus" has survived where so many other vessels have been lost. If it be so, if Captain Nemo still inhabits the oceans, his adopted country, may hatred be appeased in that savage heart.

13

A RACE AROUND THE WORLD

▼

When *Twenty Thousand Leagues under the Sea* came out in two volumes in 1869 and 1870, the critics declared it Jules's best novel so far. Early in 1870, Jules heard that he was going to receive the Legion of Honor, France's highest decoration given for outstanding service to the nation, for his writing. He was pleased and knew that his father would be even more so. Preparing the paperwork involved several delays, but finally, in July, the handsome medal arrived, and Jules took his family to Chantenay to celebrate. He and his father toasted each other far into the night. But the rejoicing didn't last long. Twenty-four hours after Jules's arrival, his mobilization orders came through. War had broken out between France and Prussia, and Jules was sent to Crotoy to set up a coast guard unit there.

The war was not unexpected. For several years, Napoleon III, emperor of France, had watched with great alarm as the independent German states had gotten together under Prussian leadership. He considered them a threat to his ambitions to dominate the continent. Jules, at the age of forty-two, knew that he was too old for soldiering, but he was surprised and pleased when the government asked him to defend the bay area against the Prussians.

In a very short time, he found himself in charge of twelve gray-haired veterans of the Crimean War who were equipped with three flintlock guns and a small cannon that was mounted on the prow of the *Saint Michel*. When it was fired, Jules thought it barked like a poodle. He couldn't help smiling to himself when he looked over his coast guard contingent that wouldn't last a minute if it ever came into contact with an enemy warship. But he vowed to do his best in defending his part of the coastline.

As the war progressed, the Prussians surged ahead in every important area. By the beginning of August, German troops had crossed the frontier and were headed for Paris. On September 1, Napoleon was captured along with 100,000 French officers and troops at Sedan. This catastrophe led to a bloodless revolution in Paris, and Napoleon, who had been emperor for eighteen years, was deposed. France soon declared itself a republic, and the new government vowed to go on with the war.

In Crotoy, news of Napoleon's downfall prompted Jules to move Honorine and the children to Amiens. By mid-September, the Germans were within sight of Paris; a few days later, they had completely surrounded the city. The new government there was determined to fight on, and a long siege began. Throughout the fall and winter of 1870, the capital kept up its resistance but finally surrendered at the end of January 1871.

During these months, Jules's little boat patrolled the bay day after day. Fortunately, it never encountered any enemy warships, and with several capable seamen taking charge of the *Saint Michel*, Jules managed to finish three novels and a short story in his floating study as the war raged on in other places.

As soon as the armistice was signed, he went to Paris several times and each time found depressing conditions and events. Many of the city's shops and cafés were shuttered and locked and the parks almost destroyed. But he wasn't prepared to hear that his cousin Henri had died from starvation. So those horror stories he had heard of the people in Paris eating the zoo animals and even rats from the sewers were true! The news devastated him, and when he discovered that Hetzel's office was closed because the publisher had gone to Monte Carlo in the south of France to escape the war, he was really depressed.

What should he do now? Here he had four manuscripts ready to be published and no one available to do it. He needed money—and soon. Should he go back to the stock exchange until the book business bounced back to normal again? He decided that it was the wise thing to do.

There was one refreshing note on one of his trips to Paris. He learned that balloons had played a great role in the war effort. More than sixty of them left the capital during the siege, with most of them landing in friendly territory carrying pigeons, dogs, and letters. One balloon flew six hundred miles to Konigsberg, Norway, while another got up to a speed of ninety-five miles an hour. Jules was elated with this news. But what really impressed him was the information that a German balloon and a French one piloted by his good friend Nadar had engaged in an air battle—the first in world history. Nadar had shot the German balloon down.

During the summer of 1871, he went back to work for a few weeks at the Bourse. During that time, he lived with his brother and Paul's wife in Paris not too far from the stock exchange. He didn't mind working there this time because he knew it would be only for the summer. Hetzel had already contacted him to tell him that he'd be ready to publish again early in the fall.

One day when he was walking home from the job, he passed Cook's Travel Agency on the boulevard and stopped to read a poster on the window. It said that the world was getting smaller and smaller and now was the time to go around the world. The Suez Canal was completed and so was the transcontinental railroad between San Francisco and New York. Thomas Cook believed that it was possible to tour the world in ninety days and challenged passersby to make the trip.

Jules's imagination took over. Could it really be done? Could a traveler make all of the right connections on time? He could picture trains and steamships rushing across continents and oceans and his hero checking his timetable again and again. Maybe there could be a wager involved to make it more exciting. And . . . why not try to do it in eighty days instead of ninety?

All of these thoughts were put on hold when Jules received word that his father was dying. He left on the next train and arrived in Nantes only a moment before Pierre Verne closed his eyes forever. Jules was grief-stricken and no doubt recalled the times the two of them didn't agree on a number of things. But he unexpectedly felt better when he heard the eulogy given by a close friend who read a letter he had recently received from M. Verne. Part of it said: "I am happy that Jules's success rests on such a solid foundation."

After the death of his father, Jules plunged into his new book, eager to begin his race around the world and to help ease his sorrow. In his study he found a piece of cardboard, drew the outlines of two figures, and cut them out. He put up a big world map on the wall, attached his figures to hat pins, and started moving them across the face of the map. Then he cut out two more cardboard figures and knew he had his four main characters.

The hero this time is Mr. Phileas Fogg, a soft-spoken English gentleman and a member of the Reform Club in London. One day at the club, playing whist, a popular card game, Fogg says that it is possible to travel around the world in eighty days. His fellow whist players laugh at him and bet him twenty thousand pounds that such a journey is impossible. Fogg, in a very calm manner, accepts the wager and prepares to leave London that very night. He will board the train for Paris at 8:45 P.M. on October 2, 1872, and will return to the Reform Club by the same time on December 21 using the following itinerary:

From London to Suez, by rail and steamboat	7 days
From Suez to Bombay, by steamer	13 days
From Bombay to Calcutta, by rail	3 days
From Calcutta to Hong Kong, by steamer	13 days
From Hong Kong to Yokohama, by steamer	6 days
From Yokohama to San Francisco, by steamer	22 days
From San Francisco to New York, by rail	7 days
From New York to London, by steamer and rail	9 days

Mr. Fogg sets out his trip accompanied by Passepartout, his faithful and witty valet, and soon a third traveler, Detective Fix, joins them. Fix knows nothing about the wager. He thinks that Fogg is a bank robber escaping from England and intends to delay him until an arrest warrant arrives.

The success of Fogg's trip depends on the train and steamship timetables he takes with him. By missing one connection he can fall behind and not get home in time. Jules, of course, creates all kinds of problems along the way. In India, for example, Fogg discovers that a fifty-mile section of railroad has yet to be built; he has to make this part of the trip by elephant. But as they trudge through the jungle, they come across a Brahmin funeral procession called a suttee. An elderly rajah has died, and his corpse is being carried on a palanquin, a kind of litter. His beautiful young wife is following on foot and will be burned alive at dawn so she can become one with her husband on his funeral pyre. This is the custom in this part of India.

Fogg is shocked when he hears of this and decides to rescue the young woman. He asks his valet to help him, and during the night they come up with an ingenious plan that frees Aouda, the Indian widow. She travels along with them and eventually becomes Phileas Fogg's great love.

In America, the travelers encounter a brawl in a wild West bar and bring about an attack by American Indians. They are held up for a while when their train going through the Rocky Mountains is faced with a bridge that can't possibly hold up if they go on it. And more time is lost when a herd of hardly moving, bewildered buffalo crosses in front of them.

Jules created one exciting episode after the other in his story of a race around the world. Near the end of the story, Mr. Fix manages to arrest Fogg and have him thrown in jail. This delay accounts for the weary travelers' arriving in London five minutes late. Not true! Not true! The wily author adds a unique twist to the tale. Since they traveled from west to east, they gained twenty-four hours as a result of the change in time zones.

When Jules had written a good basic plot and several chapters, he took them to the editor of *Le Temps,* an important newspaper in Paris. The man practically grabbed the pages and was excited by what he read. He paid Jules a goodly sum of money and begged him not to give this story to anyone else. He would run it in serial form to make his readers eager for the next chapter.

This editor, as well as others connected with *Around the*

World in Eighty Days, never dreamed it would cause the commotion it did. Newspapers in several European countries and in the United States began to run summaries of the story, blow by blow. Would Fogg make it? Soon readers on both continents made wagers on the success or failure of Fogg's venture. They were especially concerned that he might not get to New York by December 11th in order to make connection with his steamer to Europe. That would mean he couldn't possibly appear at the Reform Club in time to collect his wager. Readers throughout the world waited with great anticipation and were thrilled when Fogg succeeded.

Jules came up with one moment in America that was really terrifying. The episode occurs when they cross the Rockies on a train. Phileas learns that the suspension bridge over some rapids is so shaky that at first the engineer hesitates to go over it. But he quickly decides that with a full throttle, his train can make it—maybe. Verne writes:

The locomotive whistled vigorously; the engineer, reversing the steam, backed the train for nearly a mile —retiring, like a jumper, in order to take a long leap. Then, with another whistle, he began to move forward; the train increased its speed, and soon it rapidly became frightful; a prolonged screech issued from the locomotive; the piston worked up and down twenty strokes for the second. The passengers perceived that the train, rushing on at the rate of a hundred miles an hour, hardly bore upon the rails at all.

And they passed over! It was like a flash. No one saw the bridge.

The novel was made into a play that ran for two years in Paris and later in London, Brussels, Vienna, New York, and many other cities. Jules Verne made more money from this dramatization than from all of his books put together. But what was most pleasing to him was that after so many years he had become a successful playwright.

☞ 14 ☜

CAPTAIN NEMO RETURNS

▼

With the unbelievable success of *Around the World in Eighty Days* and the subsequent play, Jules indulged himself by buying a bigger and better boat. It was a small yacht with elegant lines, and he named it *Saint Michel II*. He also bought a mansion in Amiens, where Honorine and the children had stayed during the past two years.

He was a little reluctant to leave the sophisticated Paris area, but he believed he was doing the right thing. His two stepdaughters, Valentine and Suzanna, were growing up and had fallen in love with two young men in the city. His son, Michel, was now eleven and quite obnoxious at times. Jules had enrolled him in a strict boarding school, and he hoped this would stop him from being so wild and unruly.

He liked Amiens with its magnificent cathedral and friendly people who seemed interested in cultural things. He was pleased with his new house, which stood behind a walled garden filled with all kinds of flowers, but what really intrigued him was a stone tower on one side of the mansion. He set up his study on its second floor immediately. It had a circular window that overlooked the garden and the cathedral, and this view inspired him every morning. In this room he would write more than fifty additional extraordinary journeys.

He was pleased with its furnishings. In one corner was a comfortable leather armchair, a big globe of the world, and a camp bed. The floor was carpeted, the walls were covered with dark-flowered wallpaper, and the door had a thick, tasseled curtain on it. His reference notes, numbering more than 25,000, were crammed into several wooden cabinets and contained bits of information on everything from A to Z, literally.

Here Jules worked and often slept. He arose at 5:00 A.M. so that his actual writing, proofreading, and research were over by eleven o'clock. The best part of those six hours took place early in the morning when dawn broke over the spires of the cathedral, painting a picture worthy of the great masters. This scene from his window always motivated him to sit down at his plain wooden work table and travel in his imagination to destinations unknown.

His library lay just beyond the bedroom door, and thousands of books lined the walls, including works by his favorite poets, Homer and Vergil, as well as by Shakespeare, Montaigne, Sir Walter Scott, James Fenimore Cooper, and Charles Dickens. There was a special place in his heart for everything Dickens wrote.

Several months after moving to Amiens, he began to write a whimsical tale called *Dr. Ox's Experiment*. Jules felt wonderful. Why not try his hand at writing something lighthearted, a short novel or novella that would make readers laugh? He wanted to share this feeling of exhilaration with his loyal readers.

In the story about Dr. Ox, the town of Quiquendone in Flanders does everything in slow motion. The people there are heavy, dull, plodding, barely able to move. Dogs don't bother to bite, cats don't scratch, and conversations have many pauses. Lovers take ten years to propose and have to wait almost as long for an answer. And along comes Dr. Ox, who wants to remedy all that. He builds a gasworks for the villagers so they can have the luxury of gaslight. But it isn't gas in the pipes; it's oxygen, almost pure oxygen. The people are suddenly full of energy. Cats and dogs fight all the time, operas are rushed through in half an hour, marriages and divorces are speeded up, all laws are broken, and the jails begin to overflow. All of this frenzy comes to a halt when Dr. Ox's gasworks blows up, and the village goes back to its former lethargy.

His next novel, *The Mysterious Island*, was entirely different. Considered the best of his desert island stories, *The Mysterious Island* describes the adventures of five American men stranded on an uncharted island in the Pacific after their passenger balloon is swept away during a violent storm. The group consists of an engineer, a journalist, a black servant, a sailor, and a young student. Jules put them there to see what they could do in the face of adversity by using only their own ingenuity and what they are able to find on the island.

He definitely did not supply them with a wrecked ship from which they could use many helpful articles. That was done in *Robinson Crusoe* and *Swiss Family Robinson*. He wanted the five men to discover that if they worked together, they could create a place not only comfortable but productive.

Early in the story, Cyrus Smith, the engineer, is missing, and the other four survivors meet with one disaster after the other. The worst blow occurs when they use their last match to build a fire, and a wave comes swooping into their cave and puts it out. But the whole picture brightens when Smith is found and takes immediate command.

First of all, he shows them how to build a fire. He takes two of their watches and removes the crystals. Using clay as an adhesive, he shapes a burning glass, concentrates the rays of the sun on some dried moss, and a fire begins to burn. Then he teaches them how to make bows and arrows so they can hunt for food. Working together, they domesticate wild sheep and goats to have wool for clothing. They make wheels, build a wagon, and tame wild horses. They soon realize they must have a refuge against possible enemies or wild animals, so Smith shows them how to manufacture nitroglycerin to blast a place in a cavern. They decide to build another base at the other end of the island and connect the two. They also set up a telegraph system under Smith's guidance. As time goes on, they begin to have the comforts of civilization. Says the narrator, "It was real enjoyment to the settlers when in their room, well-lighted with candles, well-warmed with coal, after a good dinner, elderberry brew smoking in their cups, their pipes giving forth an odoriferous smoke, they could hear the storm howling without."

As time goes on, strange, mysterious things begin to happen. Smith is miraculously saved from drowning, and a pirate ship ready to land on their island is suddenly blown up. Who could be doing this? All along they have felt that someone is watching them—and over them. They receive a message one morning over their telegraph that orders them to go to a hidden entrance to a cave that opens to the sea and leads underneath the island. When they do so, they come across a little lake, and in the center is a long, cigar-shaped object. It is the *Nautilus*, and when they go aboard, they find Captain Nemo in his room looking pale and wan. He tells them that he is the one who has been watching over them. He also tells them that he is dying.

The five men stay with him for several days, and when he is on his deathbed, he relates to them some facts about his life. They learn that he is really Prince Dakkar, the son of the Rajah of Bundelkund in central India. At the age of ten, he was sent to England for schooling and after that traveled around the world. In 1849, he returned to India, married a wonderful woman, and had two children. In the mutiny of 1856, his family was slaughtered and he vowed then that their deaths would never go unpunished.

The next day he tells them that his death wish is to be buried in his boat. They answer that they will do that for him, and when he dies that night, they open the sea-cocks and the water comes rushing in. The *Nautilus* sinks slowly beneath the lake in the cavern, and Captain Nemo will now be at peace forever.

It had taken readers five years to learn the fate of Captain Nemo. At last, the secret of the enigma of Captain Nemo was solved, and readers learned some surprising facts about this strange and unhappy man.

The Mysterious Island, published in 1875 when Jules was forty-seven years old, marked a milestone in his life. From then until his death, he wrote one or two novels a year, but they couldn't compare to his earlier works.

15

A Shot in the Dark

▼

During the next ten years, from 1875 to 1885, Jules Verne wrote fifteen more fantastic voyage and adventure stories, including *Michael Strogoff,* featuring a courageous courier to the Russian czar who travels across Siberia on a secret mission; *The Begum's Fortune,* dealing with an evil scientist who could be the forerunner of Adolf Hitler; and *Matthias Sandorf,* featuring a hero patterned after Hetzel and dedicated to Alexandre Dumas, his good friend, who had died in 1870. The novel was fast-paced with many Dumas-like touches—twists, surprises, and encounters.

But in the midst of this great effort, in 1877, Jules took a break from his hectic pace and threw a party to end all parties. That March he sent invitations to seven hundred people all over France and received acceptances from three hundred and fifty. The party would be a fancy dress ball to be held at a fashionable restaurant in Amiens on April 2. He was doing this mainly for Honorine so that she would gain a place in the social circles of the city. Two days before the event, his wife became seriously ill, and Jules asked one of his stepdaughters to act as hostess.

Jules was pleased to see characters from his books, all

of whom were dressed in appropriate costumes, at the ball. He greeted Dr. Ferguson from *Five Weeks in a Balloon*, Michel Ardan of *From the Earth to the Moon*, and Professor Lidenbrock, one of the men from *A Journey to the Center of the Earth*. But he was particularly thrilled when he saw a tall, handsome man dressed as a sea captain come into the ballroom. It was, of course, Captain Nemo, and Jules shook his hand with great enthusiasm and introduced him to some of his dear friends. As he did so, he admitted that of all the characters he had created through the years, this man was his favorite. If it were possible, he would have become this sea captain, so silent and aloof and mysterious, and live at the bottom of the sea forever.

Jules came to the party as himself, looking distinguished in a dark suit and with his full reddish beard now sprinkled with gray. He entertained his guests by being witty and telling them amusing anecdotes. His close friends knew, however, that most of the time he preferred quiet evenings at home. They also realized that he was deeply concerned about Honorine during the evening but would do his best to make everyone enjoy the music and delicious food.

The next day Jules tried to get some writing done, but Honorine was still so ill that he couldn't concentrate. It took several weeks for her to begin to mend, and only then could he go to his desk. But he had another problem—Michel. He was almost seventeen and impossible to deal with. He had gotten himself into debt and become so unreasonable and incorrigible that Jules decided to put him into the town jail for a while. When Michel was allowed out, he hadn't changed a bit. This time Jules made arrangements for him to be sent to sea on a ship bound for India to work as an apprentice pilot.

Months later, when his son returned, he seemed better behaved. He couldn't resist telling his father that he often dined at the captain's table and that his "punishment" had

been more like a pleasant cruise. He hinted that the captain and crew had learned he was the son of the famous
writer Jules Verne. Michel liked the sea and signed up several more times during the next few years to work for sea
captains that Jules knew.

As time went on, Jules wrote one novel after the other,
and one day Hetzel told him to be careful, to pay more
attention to the words he put on paper. His stories were
beginning to sound mechanical, as if they were being
turned out by a machine. He reluctantly had to agree and
promised the publisher he would do his best to get away
from formula writing.

On a trip to Nantes to see his mother in 1878, he happened to see a beautiful yacht. It could carry a crew of
nine and accommodate a number of people in its luxurious cabin. Jules hesitated only a moment and bought it for
60,000 francs. He called it the *Saint Michel III* and was told
by the owner that with its powerful engines and auxiliary
sails, it could cruise around the world with the greatest of
ease.

The purchase of this handsome white yacht delighted
Jules, and he made immediate plans to go on some cruises
to get some new thoughts and ideas for several future
books. His wife and Hetzel both urged him to go. It didn't
take long for him to head for a place he had always wanted
to visit—the Mediterranean.

When he arrived there, he was surprised at the enthusiasm of the people he met. He was invited to dinners and
receptions, and no matter where he went, men and
women pressed forward to meet him and shake his hand.
Later on, he traveled to England, Scotland, and Norway,
and once again he was overwhelmed by the warm receptions he received.

In the spring of 1884, he set sail again for the blue waters
of the Mediterranean, which had become one of his favor-

ite places to visit. This cruise would be a long one, and on board were Honorine and Michel, along with his brother, Paul, and one of Paul's sons, Gaston. It promised to be a wonderful cruise. Even though Jules still worried about Michel, his son seemed more approachable lately and tried to hold his anger in check. Maybe he was finally growing up.

Jules was also pleased that his nephew had asked to come along on this trip. He was especially fond of twenty-four-year-old Gaston, who told him that he planned to record some of the happenings as they traveled. Gaston did exactly that, and from time to time he jotted down details of the people they met and the social events that took place. These items went into a school notebook he had brought along, and two of them read:

> In Vigo, the French consul met the yacht and gazed on Uncle Jules as if he were a demigod!

> In Gibraltar, the British garrisons give Verne a wonderful reception! Their officers carry him off in triumph to their mess. There, they drink punch, applaud loudly, drink more punch.[15]

Later, on the way to Malta, they ran into a violent storm, and their yacht was thrown about like a piece of driftwood. All of them were sure that it would be shattered to bits on the jagged rocks of Malta's coast. By daybreak, the storm subsided enough for a pilot to venture out in the choppy waters and guide the yacht safely to port.

In Rome, Jules was given a private audience with Pope Leo XIII, who told him he had read many of his novels and that he was impressed by their moral and spiritual value.

Their last stop was Milan. Jules wanted to study Leonardo da Vinci's fifteenth-century notes and sketches for flying machines. During the trip, he had been outlining *Robur the Conqueror*, a story that would become his most famous novel about the future of flight.

When Jules returned home, he settled down in his tower room and came back to the real world of writing and research. He wrote his Robur story, which featured a super-helicopter named the *Albatross*. When this book was finished, he spent days and nights creating *The Begum's Fortune*, which centered around the character who could have been a forerunner of Adolf Hitler. At this point in his life, he was alarmed with the thought that technology in the hands of the wrong people could ultimately destroy the world. He felt compelled to write about it so that his readers would be aware of the danger.

One night in March 1886, when *Robur the Conqueror* was appearing in installments in a well-known magazine, Jules was walking home from the Library of the Amiens Industrial Society. He had spent a pleasant afternoon there, and on his way home stopped at his club to talk to some friends. When he left them, he decided to have a soft drink at a nearby sidewalk café. He was in high spirits that day after hearing that two plays adapted from *Around the World in Eighty Days* and *Michael Strogoff* were doing extremely well at the Chatelet Theater. When it began to grow dark, he headed for home. He never saw the figure waiting there in the shadows.

As he reached the gate to his courtyard, he heard someone yell. He turned around and saw a young man running toward him waving a revolver. Suddenly, a shot rang out and a bullet struck the wall beside him. A second later, the man fired again, and this time Jules felt a searing pain in his left leg. The impact knocked him against the wall and enabled him to see his attacker.

It was Gaston, his nephew! He couldn't believe it.

☞ 16 ☜

THE FINAL JOURNEY

▼

Even as he recuperated after the shooting, Jules couldn't accept that his nephew had done such a thing. He would always remember that day with his neighbors running over to help and the police grabbing Gaston and taking him to jail. Why had he done it? Why? When Paul came to Amiens, he had an answer but not a complete one.

Paul was devastated by what had happened and told Jules that he had been worried about Gaston for months. Gaston's job as an attaché at the Ministry of Foreign Affairs was very demanding, and he had suffered a nervous breakdown several months before. But lately he had seemed fine, and Paul was sure he had recovered and could go back to his job. What, then, could have made him decide to kill an uncle he really cared about? Jealousy? Envy? A chance to be in the limelight himself? Jules was sure he would never know the true reason.

In the meantime, several doctors worked on Jules's leg, but no matter how skillfully they probed around the shinbone, they couldn't extract the bullet. Finally they said that they could save his leg but he would limp for the rest of his life. Jules was in such pain at the time that those words didn't register until several weeks later.

Jules had to endure several operations and stay in bed for three months. At first he planned to get some writing done, but the heavy doses of morphine to ease the throbbing foot and leg affected his eyesight and he couldn't see or read. In desperation, he began to create crossword puzzles, cryptograms, and acrostics to fill the empty hours, days, and weeks. By the end of his ordeal in bed, he had created hundreds of these items, most of them a cut above the average. Honorine, who hovered over him night and day, was thankful that he had a diversion to keep him busy. She realized, however, that he never stopped thinking of Gaston and what he had done.

As he began to feel a little better, he had two unexpected setbacks. He learned one morning that Hetzel had died in the south of France from a crippling disease. He knew that his publisher had not been too well the last year, but he never dreamed he was so sick. This was the man who had taken a chance on him twenty-three years ago and published his first novel. This was the man who had published every book he had ever written. How could he manage without him?

But another blow was in store. Not long after the news of Hetzel, Honorine told him that his mother had died. She was eighty-seven but had seemed in fairly good health. What made it worse was that Jules's doctor refused to let him attend the funeral. His foot was slowly healing, but he was still terribly depressed over the shooting.

That next spring he was well enough to travel to Nantes to settle his mother's estate. When he arrived at her apartment, he closed it up as well as he could, though hobbling around in shoes two sizes too big for him. He also made a trip to Chantenay, the summer home where he had spent so many happy days as a young boy. He couldn't believe the changes. In 1887 it was no longer a simple country village by the sea. Nearby Nantes had expanded and grown, and the city's industrial suburbs had come in. In a letter to a friend, Jules wrote: "The air that once used to be

JULES VERNE AT THE AGE OF SIXTY. (Courtesy of the Dublin Library)

filled with the perfume of flowers and fruit trees is corrupted now by a pall of black smoke. But what can one do? It seems that civilization must adopt the guise of hard necessity."[16]

Before leaving Nantes, Jules had one more place to visit. He had to go to his yacht, the *Saint Michel III*, which had been tied up at the dock on the riverfront. He had missed it and could hardly wait to set sail again. When he arrived, he was touched to see that some of the men had built a special gangplank so that he could get aboard the yacht without too much trouble. The devoted crew watched as he slowly and carefully headed toward them and onto the ship. He had no trouble but breathed a sigh of relief when he reached his destination. He was sure his crew did the same.

In midafternoon when the yacht sailed into the Bay of Biscay, the first sea swells came in. Jules stood stiffly on the bridge, one hand tightly grasping the railing and the other clenching the handle of his trusty cane. As the ship rolled gently, he lost his footing and fell down. The incident was over in a few minutes, and he was soon upright again, but he knew he had lost his "sea legs." Would that mean that whenever he was on a cruise and the wind came up, he would have to run into the cabin so he wouldn't topple over?

A few days later he sold the yacht, his handsome, beautiful yacht. He realized that this was a turning point in his life. He was leaving behind everything pertaining to the sea, which had been such an important part of his heart and soul. He wasn't sure how he would fill the void.

From then on Jules Verne was a different man. That didn't mean he deviated from his commitment to Hetzel to write two novels a year. His literary life saw little change. All that was new was that he now turned over his manuscripts to Pierre Hetzel's son, who had taken over the company. But many times he felt depressed and missed his family and friends who had died during the last two years. There were so many of them.

Eventually he made a change in his life so he could have some cheerful thoughts. He entered the political arena in Amiens. He was surprised when he actually was elected town councilor and pleased when the mayor assigned him to special projects. Before long he was involved in the city's educational system, the financial problems of the municipal theater, and the city's sewage disposal system.

Jules became so knowledgeable about the intricacies of running a city that he was asked by *The Forum* magazine to write an article about it. He agreed to do so and asked Michel to collaborate on the piece with him. His son, on shore from one of his stints at sea, readily agreed, and the material appeared with the two bylines in February 1889. Did Michel want to be a writer someday? He wasn't sure. Did he want to become a sailor? He didn't know. Jules vowed that he would never influence him one way or the other.

He kept on writing his novels, and once in a while he would try to do a play or a short story. But he had little enthusiasm for what he was doing. One morning his spirits were revived. A package for him came to the house, and when he opened it, he found a walking stick with a shiny gold knob at the top. The box also contained a note that said that this present was from members of the Imperial Boys' League in London. They wanted their favorite storyteller to have it so that he could use it as he continued to travel on what Jules called his extraordinary journeys.

In mid-August 1897, while he was working on one of his books, *The Superb Orinoco,* he received word that his brother Paul had suffered a series of heart attacks. A few days later, on August 22, his brother died at the age of sixty-eight. Jules, a year older, found it hard to accept.

They had always been so close, and this death was a double blow: He was losing both his brother and best friend.

During the next few years Jules developed diabetes, and he began to cut down on his activities. He still wrote several novels but had to force himself to sit down and get the writing done. Fortunately his years of self-discipline made it possible. He longed to spend a few days in Paris. He had a special reason for wanting to go: He wanted to see the Eiffel Tower, which had been completed in 1889. But somehow Jules knew he'd never see his favorite city again.

He often wished that Michel had become a writer, but his son no longer had the interest. In the recent past, Michel had married and divorced, then married for the second time a few months later. His latest letter to him said that he had a good job in the business world and that he was a contented man.

By 1903, when Jules was seventy-five, his eyesight was failing and he couldn't hear very well. His wry sense of humor made him say to Honorine: "I only run the risk of hearing half the stupid and wicked things people say. That is a big consolation."[17]

In 1903, he wrote *The Master of the World*, the sequel to *Robur the Conqueror*, in which Robur becomes a sinister man intent upon destroying the world. He plans to do so with the help of an invention that can quickly become a helicopter, a submarine, or a fast-paced car. In 1905, he gave young Hetzel material on *The Invasion of the Sea*, his last book published in his lifetime.

In March 1905, Jules became seriously ill. His diabetes had paralyzed his right side. His doctor told Honorine that he had to have absolute quiet, and when the people of Amiens heard this, they spread straw on the cobblestone streets so he couldn't hear the carriages go by. On the night of March 23, Jules's other side became paralyzed and

JULES AND HIS WIFE, HONORINE.

he whispered to Honorine to send for the family. After they arrived, he managed to give them a fond farewell look that they would always remember and cherish. A short time later, he lapsed into a coma and died at eight o'clock on the morning of March 24. He was seventy-seven years old.

His funeral was held on March 28, and more than five thousand people came, including schoolchildren, soldiers,

GOING OVER NIAGARA FALLS IN *THE MASTER OF THE WORLD.*

politicians, clergy, scientists, and writers. Memorials were later erected to him in both Nantes and Amiens. But neither one could compare to the monument that Michel raised over his father's grave in 1907. Created by the sculptor Albert Roze, it showed the bearded Verne, his hair tossed about by sea winds, breaking away from shroud and tomb and rising from the dead with a triumphant gesture. Carved on the bottom of it are his name and these words: ONWARD TO IMMORTALITY AND ETERNAL YOUTH.

EPILOGUE

▼

In 1876, a ten-year-old boy named Simon Lake read *Twenty Thousand Leagues under the Sea* while vacationing at a beach in New Jersey. He couldn't put it down and vowed that some day he would be another Nemo. That didn't really happen, but when this American was a grown man, he worked out the idea of submerging in a submarine by negative buoyancy, a technique still used today. In 1898, his *Argonaut* plunged beneath the surface of the Atlantic and traveled underwater from Norfolk, Virginia, to New York City. It became the first submarine to navigate with success in the open sea.

When Jules Verne heard of this voyage, he cabled congratulations to Simon Lake, who said that hearing from Jules Verne was the finest moment in his life. When Lake wrote a letter to a close friend, he said, "I have always maintained that Jules Verne was even more remarkable as a scientist than as a writer of romantic fiction. He had the penetrating imagination without which no inventor ever gets anywhere, coupled with an extraordinarily exact knowledge. Remarkably, the influence of Jules Verne on

THE WORLD'S FIRST NUCLEAR SUBMARINE WAS NAMED
NAUTILUS AFTER THE FICTIONAL SUBMARINE CREATED BY
JULES VERNE A CENTURY AGO. *(Courtesy of the United
States Navy)*

scientists, engineers, dreamers, and ordinary people has
continued right up to the present."

Jules Verne wrote close to one hundred books with
sixty-five of them his extraordinary journeys. Next to the
Bible and the works of Shakespeare, his are the most translated works in the world. They have been translated into
104 languages. He is known as the father of science fiction,
and his stories have made many of his readers see visions
of the future and inspired others to attain great scientific
achievements. Some of these readers are:

Norbet Casteret, a Frenchman who explored the caves and caverns of the Pyrenees to find lost lakes and dwelling places of early man.

Simon Lake, an American who was a pioneer in building submarines and navigated the first one successfully in the open sea.

Robert Goddard, an American scientist who was the father of modern rocketry and whose experiments led to the development of our space program. He believed as early as 1919 that we could put a man on the moon someday.

Wernher von Braun, a German who became an American citizen, considered the foremost rocket engineer in history, and an important contributor to America's space program.

Guglielmo Marconi, an Italian who invented the wireless telegraph and, in 1901, produced the first transatlantic wireless signal.

Admiral Robert E. Peary, the American who discovered the North Pole in 1909 and who drew encouragement from Verne's book *The Adventures of Captain Hatteras* to go on his journey to the Arctic.

Admiral Richard E. Byrd, an American, the first man to fly over the North and South Poles and who told newsmen before setting out for his third exploration to the South Pole that it was Jules Verne who brought him to that point.

William Beebe, an American naturalist and writer
whose 1934 book about his underseas adventures in
a bathysphere is called *Half Mile Down*.

Auguste Piccard, a Swiss professor who set a record
in a balloon in 1931 by remaining afloat for seventeen hours and who, in 1960, found the deepest spot
on the floor of the Pacific Ocean in a diving bell.

Yuri Gagarin, the Russian cosmonaut, who read
many of Verne's books and became the first human
to travel into space when, on April 12, 1961, he circled
the earth at a speed of more than 17,000 miles per
hour.

A number of American astronauts and space officials
who have read Jules Verne's novels, including several
stationed at the Lyndon B. Johnson Space Center in
Houston, Texas, among them Colonel Blaine Ham-
mond, an experienced pilot, who is responsible for
monitoring the status of the spacecraft *Atlantis* as it
prepares for its next flight; Richard J. Hieb, who has
qualified as a missions specialist for future space
shuttle flight crews and helped to bring in a stranded
satellite in a daring space walk in May, 1992, and Jef-
frey A. Hoffman, a researcher with an intense interest in astronomy dealing with gamma rays, who will
be working with the Italian Space Agency on a special project in 1992.

Since Jules Verne was the inventor of science fiction, you
might expect that he also has affected the lives of modern
science fiction writers. One of them is Ray Bradbury, author of *The Martian Chronicles*, *The Illustrated Man*, and
numerous other novels and stories, who says he read

Verne when he was ten, fourteen, and forty years old. In an introduction he wrote to an edition of *Twenty Thousand Leagues under the Sea,* he compared Jules Verne to Herman Melville, the author of *Moby Dick.* He drew parallels between the protagonists of these books, Captain Nemo and Captain Ahab, and between Nemo's remarkable vessel, the *Nautilus,* and the great white whale, Moby Dick.

Jules Verne also influenced Walt Disney, another visionary and adventurer. For several years Disney World featured a tour into the "jungle" inspired by *Five Weeks in a Balloon,* with the guide calling out, "Load your revolvers! It is full speed ahead for adventure. Take your last look at civilization. Not everyone returns from this trip." Disneyland now has an underwater trip aboard a "submarine" commanded by Captain Nemo.

Hollywood, of course, has profited from its contact with the works of Jules Verne. Five movies have been made from his books, and all are now available in video: *Around the World in Eighty Days, Twenty Thousand Leagues under the Sea, The Mysterious Island, A Journey to the Center of the Earth,* and *From the Earth to the Moon.*

Musicians, too, have been affected by Jules Verne's works. Rick Wakeman, a British rock star, read *A Journey to the Center of the Earth* in the 1960s and was so inspired that he wrote a musical composition of the same name, which has been recorded by the London Symphony Orchestra and the English Chamber Choir.

And in Paris, on the third floor of the Eiffel Tower, the Jules Verne Restaurant serves expensive but fabulous food.

Arthur C. Clarke, the well-known British science fiction writer and the author of *2001: A Space Odyssey,* in an introduction to an edition of *A Journey to the Center of the Earth,* wrote perhaps the most fitting tribute to the writer he and others have admired so much:

There can never be another Jules Verne, for he was born at a unique moment of time. He grew up when the steam engine was changing the material world, and the discoveries of science were changing the world of the mind. That revolution is now far behind us; we take it for granted that the future will be different from the present, forgetting that for the greater part of human history a man's way of life did not differ from his grandfather's—or his grandson's. Verne himself is one of the reasons that this is no longer true; he was the first writer to welcome change and to proclaim that scientific discovery could be the most wonderful of all adventures.

Without a doubt, Arthur C. Clarke would agree that Jules Verne deserves to be called "the man who invented tomorrow."

Bibliography

Becker, Beril. *Jules Verne*. New York: G. P. Putnam's Sons, 1966.

Born, Franz. *Jules Verne*. Englewood Cliffs, N.J.: Prentice-Hall, 1964.

Costello, Peter. *Jules Verne: Inventor of Science Fiction*. New York: Scribner's, 1978.

de la Fuye, Allotte. *Jules Verne*. New York: Coward-McCann, 1956.

Freedman, Russell. *Jules Verne: Portrait of a Prophet*. New York: Holiday House, 1965.

Kane, Robert S. *Paris at its Best*. Lincolnwood, Ill.: National Textbook Company, 1987.

Peare, Catherine O. *Jules Verne: His Life*. New York: Holt, Rinehart & Winston, 1956.

Quackenbush, Robert. *Who Said There's No Man on the Moon?* Englewood Cliffs, N.J.: Prentice-Hall, 1985.

Ross, Nancy Wilson. *Joan of Arc*. New York: Random House, 1953.

Smith, Berkely F. *How Paris Amuses Itself*. New York: Funk and Wagnall, 1903.

Verne, Jean Jules. *Jules Verne*. New York: Taplinger Publishers, 1976.

Wylie, Laurence. *Village in the Vancluse*. Cambridge, Mass.: Harvard University Press, 1961.

Notes

1. Allotte de la Fuye, *Jules Verne* (New York: Coward McCann, 1956), p. 22.
2. Jean Jules Verne, *Jules Verne* (New York: Taplinger, 1976), p. 5.
3. de la Fuye, p. 36.
4. de la Fuye, p. 32.
5. Catherine O. Peare, *Jules Verne: His Life* (New York: Holt, Rinehart & Winston, 1956), p. 61.
6. Peter Costello, *Jules Verne, Inventor of Science Fiction* (New York: Scribner's, 1979), p. 42.
7. Peare, p. 61.
8. Costello, p. 55.
9. Costello, p. 64.
10. Russell Freedman, *Jules Verne: Portrait of a Prophet* (New York: Holiday House, 1965), p. 98.
11. Beril Becker, *Jules Verne* (New York: G. P. Putnam's Sons, 1966), p. 73.
12. Verne, p. 93.
13. Verne, p. 84.
14. Freedman, p. 144.
15. Freedman, p. 169.
16. Costello, pp. 156, 157.
17. Freedman, p. 239.

Index